T0311290

The Fourth Dimension

The Fourth Dimension

THE NEXT LEVEL OF

PERSONAL AND

ORGANIZATIONAL ACHIEVEMENT

Craig Hickman
Craig Bott
Marlon Berrett
and
Brad Angus

JOHN WILEY & SONS, INC.

New York • Chichester • Brisbane • Toronto • Singapore

ISBN: 0-471-13280-2

10 9 8 7 6 5 4 3 2 1

*To four people who have made
unique contributions to this work:*

*Stanley Everett Varner
Paul Wesley Bott
Lynn Critchlow Berrett
Norman Glen Angus*

Acknowledgments

A number of people have helped make *The Fourth Dimension* a reality. Our literary agent and collaborator, Michael Snell, never wavered in his commitment and always kept us moving in the right direction, and our publisher and editor, Jim Childs, captured and expanded our initial vision, pushing us every step of the way to make the book better. The contribution of these two people qualifies them, in our view, as MetaWorkers of *The Fourth Dimension*.

We owe special thanks to Hyrum Smith and Jim Ritchie of Franklin Quest whose early support and commitment reunited the four authors. All of us had, at one time, worked together as management consultants at Arthur Young & Company, now Ernst & Young. Reunited, we began to rethink the principles, processes, and practices of performance improvement for the new world of work, an effort that eventually led to the discovery and development of the MetaWork System. Late in the process, Chris Raia helped us design the MetaWork seminar, which provided a unique opportunity to test and refine our thinking as well as make important adjustments to the book.

In addition, we thank all the people who provided invaluable assistance along the way: Mary Kowalczyk and her staff at Word-Masters for their hours of word processing; Dr. Ross Robson and Dr. Richard Kendell for their insightful review, discussion, and reference material; Pat Snell for her help in determining the proper title for the book; Winston and Jared Hickman for their thorough review and editing of the manuscript; Randy Beecraft and Mark Brown for their informed judgment on key concepts and methodologies; Kim Bott for his graphic design of the MetaWork concepts; Eric Marchant for his critique of the MetaWork assessment instruments; and Michael Silva and Terry McGann for their personal examples of MetaWorking under crisis conditions.

We owe a special debt of gratitude to the PowerWorkers, NetWorkers, ValueWorkers, and MetaWorkers in our lives who have helped us envision and articulate *The Fourth Dimension:* Julie Angus, Doris Bigio, Pam Bott, Scott Brian, Arthur Candland, Joe Cannon, Bobbie Coray, Derrick Cuthbert, Dell Fox, Mark Hoffman, Marlin K. Jensen, Tim Lyon, David S. Mathis, Dan NeVille, Brian Pittman, Scott Pynes, David Rapier, Trevor Roberts, and Cindy Yates.

Finally, we thank our families who give real meaning and purpose to our lives. Without them, this work would not have been completed.

Contents

The WorkScape
Revolution

"Work is half one's life—and the other half, too."

Erich Kastrur

BEYOND THE JOB

Stephan Snell, a 1992 graduate of Northwestern University, works in the human resources department of Nordstrom in Palo Alto, California. After majoring in communications, he went through a number of jobs, from marketing positions at the Hard Rock Cafe to corporate communications at Herzog-Hart, a pharmaceutical manufacturing company, before he found work that finally fulfilled him, both personally and financially. "For a couple of years," he says, "I spent a third of my time on the job, a third of my time sleeping, and a third of my time waiting for my life to start." Like so many of his friends, members of the so-called X generation, he had no trouble finding jobs. After all, he was a bright, responsible, well-educated young man. But his early jobs after graduation gave him little more than a paycheck. "I liked those jobs," he recalls, "but I couldn't see my life's work in any of them." Finally, his third job after college marked a turning point. "I started out selling

1

boys' apparel in the San Jose Nordstrom. I had just moved to California and I needed a job to pay my rent. Then one day, my manager suggested I apply for an opening in human resources. Though I didn't know what the job involved, it paid considerably better, so I gave it a shot." He landed the position, and, as it turned out, it suited him perfectly, enabling him to apply both his skill at establishing rapport with a wide range of people and his training in human communications. It also opened up a career that finally satisfied more than his financial needs. "Every time I recruit and train a new associate for the company," he says with no small amount of pride, "I'm making a real contribution. So many of my buddies are still draining french fries at Burger King."

Why have so many people in our society gotten stuck "draining french fries at Burger King?" How can they break out of those jobs and discover their life's work? The answers to those questions begin with an understanding of the forces that are revolutionizing the world of work.

"HEIGH-HO, HEIGH-HO, IT'S OFF TO WORK WE GO!"

How do you feel when you go to work each day? Do you, like the Seven Dwarfs in *Snow White,* whistle a happy tune? Or do you dread the very thought of your job?

Take a typical day. You wake up early and lie in bed thinking about the work that lies ahead. Before getting dressed, you work out on your *NordicTrack* while your mind struggles to discover the solution to that tough negotiation you'll wrestle with later that morning. There is so much work—so little time. You work on your relationship with your spouse or significant other; you help your children with their homework; you assist your friends in resolving their dilemmas; and you work to balance your career and your personal life. When you ponder the meaning of your life, everything comes down to work, all the physical, social, mental, and spiritual efforts that keep you in shape, earn you a living, and move you toward achieving all your goals, both personal and professional. In the broadest sense, your life *is* your work, and your work *is* your life. You'd think, then, that all of your work would inspire joy and a fulfilling sense of achievement, but, sadly, you probably associate the word more with backaches and migraines than with joy and fulfillment.

Your morning paper tells the sad story of displaced workers, underemployed single mothers, and young unemployed college graduates who find themselves trapped in a world of low-paying dead-end jobs. You shake your head over an unending stream of headlines announcing one major corporate layoff after another, plant closings, relocations, downsizings, unemployment rates that remain high after recessions, negotiated pay reductions, and the elimination of once-sacred employee benefits. Articles in your favorite magazines advise displaced workers to put their careers and lives back on a meaningful track. Television reports show career counselors urging college graduates to learn new skills and outplacement specialists telling how feverishly they work to turn up new employment possibilities for the victims of downsizing.

There seems to be work, work, everywhere, but little joy in sight. Not so long ago, certain futurists were predicting reduced work weeks and an abundance of leisure time. They were wrong. The high-paying, soul-satisfying, lifetime-secure job has joined the spotted owl on the list of endangered species. Perhaps, some experts argue, the demise of conventional job security opens up exciting opportunities. Scramble to rebuild your security, they propose. Make yourself more valuable and productive. If you follow their advice, however, you may come to discover that your valiant efforts only result in you doing the work of two, thus eliminating yet another job, perhaps even your own. A revolution is certainly underway, but somehow people have not yet found ways to harness all the changes for their benefit.

While researching and writing this book, we've talked with hundreds of business people all over the world. Without exception, executives, managers, and employees everywhere see massive changes occurring in the way people and organizations work. Their observations include these:

3

- If people don't continuously update their skills, they will contribute increasingly less to their organizations.

- The next wave of work activity will move beyond profit maximization or even value creation to global stewardship.

- People should prepare themselves to change jobs or contract work assignments more often and more quickly than in the past.

- Organizations will begin publishing extensive directories that not only describe what employees do, but also what specialized knowledge, skills, experience, insight, and other capabilities they possess.

- Work in the future will be defined only by those performing it, not by those managing or overseeing it.

- As the global economy gets bigger, the smallest players will become more powerful.

- The secure job will become riskier, whereas freelance work will become more secure.

- Organizations will spend much less time worrying about finding the right leadership and a lot more time worrying about spreading the right stewardship or shared responsibility to everyone, including outsourcing partners.

- Talent, motivation, and temperament will contribute more to success in the workplace than education, experience, and recommendations.

- Developing "maps" of every kind—knowledge maps, information maps, talent maps, work process maps, relationship maps, and customer maps—will prove vital when over half of an organization's workers hold their positions temporarily.

- Partnerships of every conceivable type and configuration between individuals, teams, and organizations (rather than hierarchy, command, and control) will rule the day.

- Because work that is little more than a source of income, stress, and pain cannot last, the future must provide more meaningful, fulfilling, and joyful opportunities.

- Sabbaticals taken by full-time, temporary, or contract employees to explore issues, concerns, and subjects of particular interest will characterize the next decade.

- The old world of work is giving way to a new world of work, with all of the evidence pointing to the massive shift in American work patterns and traditions that has already created a situation in which 35 percent of the work force holds part-time, temporary, or contractual jobs, or does not work at all.

All of these prognostications derive from a few basic forces that are revolutionizing the WorkScape: the demise of the conventional job and traditional hierarchical management, the continuance of globalization, the explosion of technology advancement, and the emergence of a new information economy, all of which conspire to produce an awesome force for change. The old order is dying out, but what will replace it?

BURYING THE OLD ORDER

With downsizing, streamlining, outsourcing, and reengineering programs proliferating among companies driven by the need to compete effectively in the dog-eat-dog world marketplace, a paradox has emerged. On the one hand, employers have been eliminating jobs and job security, reducing compensation and restricting benefits, while on the other hand, they have begun seeking greater employee commitment through such programs as total quality management, employee empowerment, and self-directed work teams. To their credit, those who manage today's work force increasingly recognize a need for a closer partnership between employer and employee, a partnership wherein both share the risks, responsibilities, and rewards of prosperity. The tougher the going gets, they believe, the more they should value a partnership with employees that stresses responsibility for results, not just a job. So, where does that leave the individual worker who feels pulled apart by the seemingly warring forces of less security but more commitment?

The resolution to that paradox lies in reshaping the very heart of the relationship between employer and employees by developing a new psychological contract—the unwritten, but mutually understood and accepted agreement between employer and employee that they will treat each other fairly—encompassing the ideas of empowerment, total quality, line of sight, whole system design, self-discovery learning, and team destiny. It stands to reason that as conditions in society and the workplace change, then the *psychological contract* must also change. The revolution in the WorkScape has broken the old contract and has created a climate that demands a totally new one. It happened before, during the Industrial Revolution, when everything about the American work environment changed dramatically. As industrial development matured and the organized labor movement stabilized, employees found themselves individually less important and far less independent, a turn of events that forged a psychological contract that resembled what Willie Loman expressed in *Death of a Salesman:* "If I work hard and fast and remain loyal to the company, I will always have a job, and the company will take care of me." By working hard and fast within the strict parameters defined by a job description, employees guaranteed their security. One's skills got one hired. What happened after hiring, in terms of skills development and advancement, depended on the employer's benevolence as much as on the employee's own effort. Employers based decision making on a hierarchical structure that generally defined the formal nature of working relationships on the job. Any attempt by an employee to circumvent the structure usually resulted in a reprimand or job loss. Although employers paid lip service to innovation and creativity over the years, and even rewarded those traits at times, such characteristics seldom appeared in any definition of an employee's job responsibility. The value an individual employee added to the work product generally occurred within the parameters of his or her job description. Today, all that is changing. The job no longer provides a viable way of organizing work, and in its place has arisen adaptable work units, interdependent teamworkers, results-based assignments, and shared responsibility. Table I.1 outlines the key differences between the preindustrial, industrial, and postindustrial eras.

Like the eighteenth-century workers who wrestled with the effects of a dying agrarian society and an encroaching industrial revolution, late twentieth-century workers struggle with the effects of a dying industrial revolution and an emerging postindustrial society. In the midst of this current struggle, we see the need for a whole new approach to work, one that will reinvent

Table I.1. Key differences among work eras

Preindustrial Era	Industrial Era	Postindustrial Era
Small work units	Large work units	Adaptable work units
Independent workers	Dependent workers	Interdependent workers
Occasional change	Frequent change	Constant change
Little job structure	Highly structured jobs	Results-based assignments
Personal relationships	Vertical, rigid hierarchies	Shared responsibility

the dialogue between employer and employee in a way that focuses on performance and contribution, one that will, in the end, put the joy back into work. That new approach should adhere to timeless principles so fundamentally sound that they can transcend all circumstances and enable all people to succeed both financially and personally.

The new psychological contract might go something like this: "The organization cannot offer you total job security. Your employment will depend upon your ability to add value to the organization. The organization will provide the freedom, resources, and training for you to do your valuable work, and it will pay you according to your contribution." That may sound a bit threatening, but what a world of opportunity it opens up! Your future depends on one thing only: *the value of your own contribution.*

FORGING THE NEW ORDER

In 1957, Ayn Rand published her masterwork, *Atlas Shrugged,* in which her ideal, fully integrated, near-perfect main character, John Galt, withdraws from the world because he refuses to support those who will not perform or produce for themselves. When Galt's "strike of the producers" brings the world's productivity to a standstill, he details his new philosophy, proclaiming that, "Productive work is the process by which man's consciousness controls his existence, a constant process of acquiring knowledge and shaping matter to fit one's purpose, of translating an idea into physical form, of remaking the earth in the image of one's values—your work is yours to choose, and the choice is as wide as your mind—nothing more is possible to you and nothing less is human." In the end, John Galt's refusal to live in a world where producers support nonproducers sets the stage for Ayn Rand's vision of a new American Dream in which individuals assume full responsibility for producing value and creating their futures.

A few years later, in the early 1960s, John Gardner stressed this same timeless key to a healthy, prosperous society in his bestselling book, *Excellence.* The future, he wrote, depends on "a pervasive and almost universal striving for good performance." Gardner argued that the performance of individuals, groups, departments, corporations, institutions, and nations shapes their ultimate security, self-esteem, and fulfillment. However, while Ayn Rand's novel and John Gardner's treatise depict dreams of a better world, neither offers a practical guide for making those dreams come true. Rand and Gardner were idealists, but the words of idealists do not change the world unless a concrete system translates their words into action that people can actually apply to their daily lives.

Now, more than ever before, individuals feel less subject to governments, corporations, dogmas, institutions, schools of thought, and tradition. The stage is now set for a new order, a new system that can simultaneously improve corporate results and enable individuals to prosper in their individual careers. However, individuals and organizations must dramatically improve their performance and contribution to thrive in the new order. Otherwise, they will find themselves crushed under the wheels of the new economy—ruthless global competition, lightning-fast change, tremendous environmental and resource constraints, and rivals who offer "best in world" performance. Today's blossoming technology enables individuals to think of themselves as self-contained small businesses, unique self-directed forces, whether individual or organizational, that can and will shape the future of enterprise.

However, technology, which helps people do more for less, does not provide the final answer. Although it may help someone attain a higher level of productivity, it doesn't supply enough power on its own to shape the new order, including the new psychological contract between employers and employees. As the German philosopher, Arthur Schopenhauer, observed in 1851, "Every man takes the limits of his own field of vision for the limits of the world." Men and women act, or are acted upon, according to their views of work and life. To enlarge people's field of vision with a broader, deeper definition of performance and contribution, we have developed the Meta-Work System,™ a practical guide to prospering after the WorkScape revolution. With it, individuals, teams, and organizations can

- Do more with less to produce the right *results* through *PowerWorking* (the First Dimension of Work).

- Develop greater individual and collective *competence* with *NetWorking* (the Second Dimension of Work).

- Discover more frequent *breakthroughs* that have greater impact by *ValueWorking* (the Third Dimension of Work).

- Determine a more fulfilling and meaningful *destiny* through *MetaWorking* (the Fourth Dimension of Work).

All revolutions are followed by periods of relative stability, of course, but when you're standing in the midst of a tornado of change, it is hard to see what the world will look like after the storm has subsided. The MetaWork System™ provides a road map to the world of work after the current revolution, and it gives you the know-how you'll need to control your own destiny in the relative calm after the storm, as well as position yourself for future revolutions.

CHAPTER ONE

The MetaWork
System

"So much of what we call management
consists of making it difficult for people to work."

Peter Drucker

No contemporary industry changes with more speed than the computer industry. So, if you want to keep ahead of the pack, you must change your company's values and objectives just as speedily, no? No. Lewis Platt, CEO of Hewlett-Packard (HP), has chosen, instead, to reemphasize the *HP Way* that Bill Hewlett and Dave Packard inaugurated in 1957. In recent years, it seems, the company began drifting away from its initial principles by stressing business results at the expense of people development.

Platt wants HP to retain its best people, something he knows it cannot do with money alone. People more often leave one company for another because they yearn for individual development as much as they do for compensation. Because developing and growing people fuel the kind of innovative breakthroughs that have always characterized the HP Way, Platt has made renewal and rebalancing of the company's original values and objectives a top priority for the $25 billion computer company.

Managers throughout HP follow the new *Manager's Guide to the HP Way,* which promotes the company's original values:

Trust and Respect for the Individual
High Achievement and Contribution
Integrity   *Do these values*
Teamwork   *look familiar?*
Flexibility and Innovation

Corporate objectives haven't changed since 1957, either:

Profitability
Customer Satisfaction
Fields of Interest   *Do these goals sound*
Growth   *similar to your own*
People Development   *company's objectives?*
Management Effectiveness
Citizenship

The HP Way rebalancing act requires managers to get more involved in teaching, implementing, and living the HP Way. Platt and other HP executives hope such initiatives will help keep Hewlett-Packard among the most admired companies in the world.

Interestingly, HP figured out the fundamentals in the 1950s, but the company now understands more than ever before that keeping all the fundamentals properly focused and integrated poses today's and tomorrow's biggest challenge.

METAWORKING

MetaWorking involves choosing the right dimension of work in order to produce an ever-improving track record of results, competence, and breakthroughs.

THREE-DIMENSIONAL THINKING

In 1966, Lyle Anderson, a serial punch machine operator at the IBM card manufacturing plant in Greencastle, Indiana, used an ordinary paper clip to engineer a companywide revolution. The Greencastle plant closed in the mid-1970s after magnetic tape, then disks, replaced the old punched card system for computer data processing, but back in the 1960s the plant turned out millions of cards each year for customers worldwide, including the U.S. Treasury. Lyle was a farmer who had taken a job at the card plant to provide a steady income for his family. He operated an Automatic Serial Punch Machine (ASPM), which punched slots onto the faces of serially numbered 3" × 8" paper cards. Operating at full speed, the machine drove a blur of cards from a tray in front to a stacking mechanism at the rear, but it almost never ran at full speed because its very operation tended to alter the alignment of cards as they traveled through the machine. Even a minor misalignment for a few minutes would result in several hundred defective cards the computer couldn't read. Sometimes, the department seemed to scrap more cards than it shipped.

Lyle Anderson was a slim, sandy-haired young fellow who could take a John Deere tractor apart and put it together without getting his hands dirty. Nothing bothered him more than a piece of machinery that didn't hum like a top, so he studied his clattering serial punch machine, picked the brains of other ASPM operators, and lay awake at night pondering the problem—the vibration of the ASPM caused a mechanism that held the card for the punching device to shift out of alignment. Finally, he came up with an ingenious solution: a simple spring that would withstand the vibration. Showing up early for work one morning, he took a steel paper clip and bent it this way and that until, voilá, his machine produced perfectly punched cards at twice the pace of other ASPMs on the shop floor.

Although second nature to him, Lyle's approach to the problem encompassed three basic dimensions of work—Doing PowerWork, Developing NetWork, and Discovering ValueWork. He *did* PowerWork by always striving for efficiency and effectiveness, he *developed* NetWork by sharpening his own skills and relating them to others, and he *discovered* ValueWork by inventing something that made a lasting contribution. He was, in short, a MetaWorker encouraged by an IBM environment that rewarded original thinking, teamwork, and individual productivity. Throughout the Greencastle plant, management had posted the famous IBM THINK signs, and at regular company meetings, managers urged workers to come up with ideas that could increase productivity and profitability. If a worker invented something that worked, IBM would apply that invention worldwide and compensate its inventor based on resultant cost savings or increased earnings.

In 1967, after the company had installed Lyle Anderson's anti-shimmy device in ASPM machines in plants in the United States and overseas, Lyle's manager presented him with a check for more than $36,000, three times his annual take-home pay.

While Lyle Anderson's unheralded accomplishment took place long before the new realities of reengineering, corporate downsizing, globalization, and accelerated technological change, it offers a timely, yet timeless, lesson: Real success comes not just from working harder or working smarter but from working in a way that creates value far beyond your own private corner of the world.

METAWORK: PUTTING THREE-DIMENSIONAL THINKING TO WORK

Imagine yourself working at home in the future, positioned in front of your teleputer workstation, simultaneously serving three

THREE-DIMENSIONAL THINKING	
The First Dimension	Doing
The Second Dimension	Developing
The Third Dimension	Discovering

different company divisions on contract. During a typical day you navigate the Internet looking for new and unusual "best practices"; formulate a product launch strategy in concert with three other people located in London, Singapore, and Cairo; test-run a groupware CD-ROM training program with 20 people scattered across Europe; and interview a dozen global customers to better align service offerings and segment needs. Your future in the new wired world and global economy depends on the power, meaning, and value of your contribution today and every day from now on. But precisely how do you go about making yourself more powerful, meaningful, or valuable?

Increasing your contribution takes much more than the same old approach to work—*producing more for less,* the traditional, yet one-dimensional, approach that emphasizes becoming more effective and efficient. Becoming more valuable in today's world means going beyond effectiveness and efficiency, as Lyle Anderson did, and embracing a new broader, more three-dimensional way of thinking about physical, social, and mental effort. Three-dimensional thinking can result in what we call MetaWork, and it can make individuals, teams, and organizations more powerful, united, and valuable than ever before.

Just as any object occupies the three dimensions of space (horizontal, vertical, and longitudinal), the physical, social, and mental activity of any individual, team, or organization operates in three dimensions of work (doing, developing, and discovering). Each dimension represents a different concept of work. When you, your team, and/or your organization operate in all three dimensions, moving from one to another whenever necessary, you are performing MetaWork (Fig. 1.1). The *Atlanta Braves* finally won a World Series, after 40 years and two recent opportunities, because they performed, under the wise direction of Bobby Cox, a better job of blending their game plan (Value-Work), teamwork (NetWork), and execution (PowerWork).

Whenever people engage in an activity—physical, social, mental, or spiritual—they enter a multidimensional world. Although most people understand the PowerWork dimension, constantly striving to become more effective and efficient in order to increase results, many neglect the other two dimensions.

Figure 1.1. MetaWork: working in the fourth dimension.

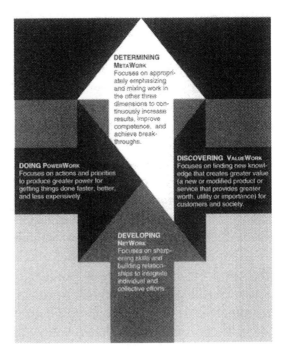

The hustle and bustle, hyperactivity of American culture keeps them constantly running in place. As early as the 1830s, well-known writers such as Frenchman Alexis de Tocqueville noted, "It is strange to see with what feverish ardor [Americans] pursue their own welfare, and to watch the vague dread that constantly torments them lest they should not have chosen the shortest path which may lead to it." A growing proportion of Americans feel in a hurry, succumbing in ever greater numbers to an old, but ever more debilitating disease—excessive activity syndrome. This "activity sickness" robs people of the other two dimensions of work, Developing NetWork and Discovering ValueWork. A middle manager at American Express during a recent one-day retreat expressed an increasingly common lament, "I feel like I'm working more and contributing less. It's the busy-work thing. Somehow, I've got to do something different."

The continuing rash of news stories on overworked Americans, stressed-out employees, burned-out bosses, downsizing blues, workaholism, time-squeezed relationships, and neglected children underscores the phenomenon of people running in place without making progress. A comparison of labor statistics spanning from 1970 to 1990 reveals that the average American adult works more hours today than in the past—163 more hours per year to be precise. That's a month's worth of doing more work, but it's seldom a month spent developing new talents and relationships, much less discovering new knowledge and innovation. The increase in work hours seems to promote excessive activity syndrome, which may explain much of the growing hollowness and emptiness many people experience at work, where they race through the day, yet go home weary and unfulfilled. It may also explain why most organizations find it so hard to inspire and empower their people. Certainly, more and more managers pay lip service to the notion that "our employees are our most valuable asset," but the new social contract between employers and employees makes it clear that "if you don't redesign the way you work, to do more with less, you're fired. Oh, and by the way, while you're at it, you'd better become more innovative, risk-taking, visionary, and committed to the organization's goals." Ironically, the so-called new economy of downsizing, cost-cutting, work system redesigning, performance-worshipping, and steadily mounting pressure for tangible results in an increasingly competitive world makes it virtually impossible for people to work beyond the PowerWork dimension. No one knows the exact price people and organizations pay for America's obsession with doing at the expense of developing and discovering, but the dilemma does invite a few tough questions:

- How many innovations have eluded people who were too tired to look for them?

- How many challenges have overprogrammed workers ignored?

- How many bad decisions have people made because they were too pressed to consider other alternatives?

- How many people have been overstressed, burned-out, disillusioned, frustrated, and destroyed because their organizations worried only about gaining more short-term results at less cost?

For too many people, working in the second and third dimensions—Developing NetWork and Discovering Value-Work—becomes a "hit or miss," even "mystical," proposition. However, without understanding exactly how to sustain and maximize work in all three dimensions, most people can expect only mediocre results, partial fulfillment, and fleeting success. Let's examine the three dimensions of MetaWork more closely.

THE FIRST DIMENSION: DOING POWERWORK

Lt. Col. Robert Fitch frowned as he stepped out of Wing Commander Col. James McCracken's office. McCracken commanded the 509th Bombardment Wing, which, among other distinguished accomplishments, had flown the historic Enola Gay atomic bomb mission during World War II. Fitch had just learned from McCracken that the Eighth Air Force had reduced his Squadron's allotted flying hours by 10 percent.

An anxious Fitch walked down the hall to his next meeting with Col. "Mad Jack" Harris, the 509th's Director of Operations and Col. McCracken's right-hand man, the one responsible for directing all flying operations in the wing. A standing joke among the flying crews went like this: How many times had Mad Jack ejected from a plane? Once too many? Or once to few? Fitch's meeting with Col. Harris began like most of Mad Jack's meetings, straight to the point.

"Fitch, even though your squadron's flying hours have been reduced, everyone, and I repeat everyone, will remain current in their flying requirements. No one will drop dead (become noncurrent), unable to 'sit alert' (be able to fly their emergency war order mission). Do I make myself clear?"

"Yes sir," Fitch saluted, turned, and left the office.

Fitch's squadron, the 509th AREFS (Air Refueling Squadron), flew KC-135 Tankers (Boeing 707s) on air refueling assignments anytime and anywhere an aircraft required fuel. Whether in war or peace, these assignments required that all crews (pilot, copilot, navigator, boom operator) maintain a 100 percent skill level in their specialties. Because a refueling mission demanded precise timing, positioning, and skill, every crew practiced and repracticed every potential variety of the refueling mission. A slipup by any crew member could spell disaster for the KC-135, the receiving airplane, or both.

Fitch assembled his training and scheduling team for the squadron: Majors Fluery, Woods, and Dubois; Lt. Angus; and Sgt. Huddleston. As he relayed the news, the team immediately realized they would have to start doing a lot of things differently. Fitch concluded the meeting by saying, "These cutbacks in flying time are probably a way of life for the near future. One of this team will 'sit alert' for any crewdog (crew member) that goes noncurrent." Sitting alert meant spending seven days at the end of the runway in a poorly furnished dormitory, nicknamed the "minimum security prison," waiting for the signal horn that would send the crew running to fulfill its EWO (Emergency War Order) Mission. Needless to say, none of the training and scheduling team wanted to sit more alert than necessary.

The team's first problem involved keeping 51 crews (204 people) and 14 airplanes scheduled in such a way that everyone would stay current. Staying current meant that every 90 days, crewdogs practiced certain events such as instrument landing, celestial navigation, and night boom refueling, in order to retain full proficiency. For starters, the training and scheduling team began specifying the events that each crew member would perform on a given flight instead of leaving it up to the crew member, as had been the previous custom. In the past, a crew member that was about to drop dead would join any other near-noncurrency crew members on a special currency flight. Unfortunately, the 10 percent cutback in flying time eliminated that option.

In the downsized program, the training and scheduling team held weekly meetings at which they studied computer printouts for each crew member, prepared the night before at no small irritation to the records department. The first scheduling meetings lasted all day long and provided the raw material for endless jokes. How many officers does it take to schedule a training flight? Thirteen? Twelve to carry the printouts, and one to stare at the scheduling board. The training and scheduling team would show up with all the computer printouts and begin studying the 6- by 20-foot scheduling board, not knowing where to being. Up to this point, training and scheduling had simply involved matching available crews with projected missions. Everyone flew plenty of missions, and anyone could always get on a special flight if needed. Now, with no more special flights and with flying hours drastically reduced, the officers had to plan every mission carefully to include the required crew members to keep them current.

Slowly but surely, the training and scheduling team figured out new ways to put more current status events into each flight, using new data summarization techniques, coordination meetings with other divisions in the wing, and innovative policies to maximize the productivity of all crews and flight equipment. By mixing and matching crews and flights, the group managed to make the most of its limited flying time. They even lobbied and got permission from headquarters to practice currency events after other missions, something no one would have dreamed of doing before.

After the first month, the scheduling meetings took only two hours, and by the end of the first quarter, the 509th AREFS had met all the training and scheduling objectives. Few other Air Refueling Squadrons in the 8th Air Force had done so. Wing Commander Col. James McCracken personally gave the training and scheduling team a big "Atta-Boy" for the effort, but immediately afterward, Major Fluery reminded Lt. Angus, "Put that Atta-Boy with the rest of them you have received, but never forget that one screw-up removes a thousand Atta-Boys." Lt. Angus can still remember feeling an odd blend of accomplishment and emptiness after the major's comment. The team had worked hard to meet the challenge of the 10 percent cut in flying time, but a few weeks later, they were ordered to cut flying hours by another 10 percent. Lt. Angus wondered whether it would ever end. He realized for the first time in his life that doing powerful work, although vitally important to any organization because it produces much needed effectiveness and efficiency, never quite gets the job done.

THE ESSENCE OF POWERWORK

Most people think of PowerWork as "getting things done" or "making things happen." PowerWork involves doing the right things (effectiveness) and doing them the right way (efficiency) to produce results.

- PowerWorkers are motivated by doing work better, faster, and cheaper; they often exhibit traits such as an action bias, strong goal orientation, and practical realism.

- People who excel at PowerWork usually exhibit a superior ability to organize activity, improve performance, and maximize results.

- The PowerWorker's secret to improvement lies in continuously measuring, benchmarking, and redesigning everything.

- PowerWorkers constantly ask one question, "What should I *do* now?"

According to this concept, the Egyptians performed PowerWork when they built the pyramids, moving massive blocks of stones some distance and assembling them to form breataking structures. It took 100,000 people working every day during the flood season (3 months per year) for 20 years to accomplish the feat. Today, if several people gather at the side of the Great Pyramid of Cheops and put their shoulders against it for an hour but fail to budge it, they have not done any work. Powerful work does not occur unless it gets things done. All that you do on the job every day may make you tired by the time you go home, but if you cannot measure "getting things done," you have not really done any PowerWork. Ted Waitt didn't make that mistake.

Thirty-one-year-old Ted Waitt, CEO of $1.7 billion Gateway 2000, built his entire operation on the idea of becoming more efficient. In the mid 1980s, Waitt started his company in Sioux City, Iowa, with the goal of making it easier for customers to combine computers, printers, and monitors. Popularizing what's now called PC bundling, Waitt did, in fact, make it easier and more efficient for customers to pick a complete system from Gateway's catalogue. In the process, Gateway became the largest direct seller of PCs in the United States. When competitors began duplicating Gateway's approach, Waitt stayed focused on remaining efficient by outsourcing everything except his core competencies—marketing and service. Today, he ruthlessly cuts costs that don't directly improve marketing or service, he always keeps inventory as lean as possible, he religiously rewards people only for performance, and he constantly thinks of new ways to increase efficiency.

PowerWork has provided the mainstay of corporate productivity ever since Adam Smith's invisible hand of the marketplace clasped the visible hand of management in the first era of modern management, just after the turn of the century. Business owners and executives, Henry Ford among them, pushed the prevailing industrial doctrine of the "economic man" to its limits. As Ford himself insisted, "The man who puts in a bolt does not put on the nut; the man who puts on the nut does not tighten it." Unfortunately, such an attitude reduced people in large- and mid-sized industrial companies to interchangeable production process units that executives needed merely to analyze, quantify, and manipulate in order to increase efficiency. While this mentality did lead to significant increases in productivity through efficiency, it also fueled the labor union movement in the United States as workers united to demand, among other things, that the managements of the mass production industries fulfill employees' needs to people and stop treating them as interchangeable disposable units of the production line. Although managers did start paying more attention to morale and work conditions, they did so only to boost efficiency, and their relationships with workers remained markedly adversarial. Remember Lyle Anderson and the Greencastle IBM card factory? In the summer of 1965, the Teamsters Union attempted to organize the plant's workers and stood outside the gates passing out flyers promising to "eradicate unfair working conditions." With a check for $36,000 in his lunch pail, Lyle wadded up the flyer and tossed it over his shoulder. Not one IBM worker signed up with the union, and the union organizers were all but tarred and feathered and run out of town on a rail.

THE MATURING OF POWERWORK

Since the mid-1960s, a renewed focus on effectiveness has spawned innumerable management fads and techniques. Executives looking for a competitive edge have ridden the waves from corporate structure to strategy, culture, innovation, leadership, quality, and transformation, refining and modifying each new fad before embarking, through vision or force, onto yet another new program. The disastrous consequences of poor implementation of one fad after another has finally brought management back to the basics of work flow and design.

After a decade of emphasis on total quality, customer satisfaction, employee empowerment, and team building, the concept of reengineering seemed to synthesize the essence of effectiveness—doing more right work and less wrong work. According to Michael Hammer and James Champy, authors of the best-selling *Reengineering the Corporation,* "For 200 years people have founded and built companies around Adam Smith's brilliant discovery that industrial work should be broken down into its simplest and most basic tasks. In the postindustrial business age, corporations will be founded and built around the idea of reunifying those tasks into coherent business processes." At the heart of this concept of reengineering lies a simple idea: You must reengineer every process in your organizations in fundamental, radical, dramatic, and revolutionary ways to achieve greater effectiveness, or PowerWork. It's a "start from scratch" approach to work that helps us to eliminate wrong or unnecessary work and then figure out how to group and combine the right work in order to accomplish major, rather than incremental, improvements.

While concepts like reengineering have helped PowerWork mature over the years, work achievements in this dimension still aim merely at getting more results for less cost, and most efforts toward that end ignore the other two dimensions of work. Obviously, everyone needs to work more powerfully, but doing so without harnessing the other two dimensions can only produce relatively minor improvements in productivity. Success in the new economy hinges on going beyond PowerWork to NetWork.

THE SECOND DIMENSION: DEVELOPING NETWORK

In 1985, Thomas Craig, then consulting manager with Arthur Young International, now Ernst & Young, found a business opportunity at the Idaho National Engineering Laboratory (INEL). The lab wanted to benchmark its scientific research performance with "best in class" competitors, but now knowing much more about benchmarking than that it sounded vaguely scientific, they began looking for an outside consultant who could facilitate the process. To Craig, this looked like a wonderful opportunity for Arthur Young, so he set his sights on winning the contract. "I realized," he remembers, "that most of the competitors for the project could easily demonstrate their ability to conduct state-of-the-art competitive analyses and even stretch their capabilities to fit the unique needs of this project, so I quickly began looking for someone within the firm who had actually conducted competitive benchmarking studies."

At the time, Arthur Young had built a corporate culture around competence and team building, whose consulting managers such as Craig could assemble teams of consultants with the competencies required by a project from anywhere in the firm, even from the ranks of partners and senior executives. Because the firm's culture stressed the "marketability" of such flexible teams, everyone in the firm continually marketed their unique competencies throughout the organization. The entire system focused on individuals sharpening their skills and integrating those skills with others to serve clients' special needs.

Tapping into this system, Craig first examined the firm's extensive internal data bank of professionals worldwide. The listing detailed the education and professional background of individuals, as well as their unique fields of expertise and experience. In short order, Craig identified those with the range of skills he believed he needed for the INEL benchmarking project, including industrial engineers, consultants who had worked in research and laboratory settings, strategists, and financial analysts. To his dismay, however, he could not find anyone with the competitive benchmarking experience he sorely needed. Relying then on his own informal network within the firm, a network he had continually nurtured over the years, he thought about all the people with whom he had worked on past projects, peers he had met at conferences, and partners throughout the organization. He knew he could trust these people because they understood that a project team's success depended on their ever-growing skills and the blending of those skills behind a common purpose. After three phone calls, Craig found Francis K. Jones, a new member of the firm, working out of the New York City office. Prior to joining Arthur Young as a partner in the area of competitive strategy, Jones had worked for Xerox Corporation, where he had spearheaded the company's competitive benchmarking efforts. Jones eagerly joined Craig's INEL team.

Given Craig's superior ability to assess client needs and match them with consultant competencies, he became team leader, even though he lacked specific expertise in the field of benchmarking. With the addition of Jones to the team, he believed he could convince INEL that Arthur Young could do a better job than anyone else competing for the assignment. It worked. INEL awarded Arthur Young the competitive analysis and benchmarking engagement, the results of which allowed INEL to greatly improve its operation.

The success of Craig and the Arthur Young team illustrates the benefits of including both the first and second dimensions of work on a project. They did PowerWork, but they also developed NetWork by sharpening their skills and building relationships with others in a way that integrated individual and collective efforts.

THE ESSENCE OF NETWORK

While on the surface NetWork involves "maintaining vital relationships," "forging common purpose," or "building unity amid diversity," on a deeper level it involves *developing* skills and relationships that unite individual and collective efforts. For example:

- NetWorkers, motivated by nurturing talent, continually build relationships with other people that fully tap the potential of all involved; they communicate clearly and persuasively, forging unity amid diversity.

- People who excel at NetWorking demonstrate superior ability to develop people, build common purpose, and deploy talent.

- The NetWorker's secret to improvement lies in continuously selecting, cultivating, and partnering with the right people.

- NetWorkers constantly ask the question, "Where should I focus my *development* efforts now?"

If all we do at work every day fails to sharpen new or existing skills and create unity among people, we have not really developed any NetWork. Steve Wiggins didn't fall into that trap.

Steve Wiggins, the 37-year-old CEO of Oxford Health Plans, keeps actively involved in every competitive sports activity imaginable—shooting hoops, taking in a round of golf, playing a few sets of tennis, pitching for a city softball team, road racing, entering a bicycle competition, fly fishing in Ontario, you name it. So what does Steve's restless energy reveal about NetWork? A lot, it turns out. Wiggins thrives on change. "In business you're thrown a different curve ball every day," says Steve. "If you're going to succeed, you have to figure out a way to think about change." His talent for discerning shifts and turns, sizing up opportunities, building critical relationships with vital stakeholders, and creating unconventional initiative in the rapidly changing health care market has given Oxford tremendous competitive advantage, making it one of the fastest-growing HMOs in the United States. Revenues rose to $312 million last year, double the previous year, and Wall Street analysts predict it will reach $1 billion by 1995. In response to quality-conscious East Coast customers, Wiggins enlists only the best doctors and dentists, lets patients choose between their own doctors or managed-care network doctors, quickly adds new services, and aggressively takes risks. He expects his latest move— establishing a separate company to help independent doctors survive the managed-care upheaval by organizing into a variety of cost-saving groups—to pay off big.

The second dimension of work delivers results because it strikes at the heart of the timeless concern with the development of talent and the attainment of a common purpose. Until now, this dimension of work has resisted clear definition. Even General Electric CEO Jack Welch expresses his own uncertainty about maximizing productivity in this vital dimension. "I think any company that's trying to play in the 1990s has got to find a way to engage the mind of every single employee. Whether we make our way successfully down this road is something only time will tell—but I'm sure this is the right road." Engaging every employee depends on creating an organization without boundaries, a structure that erases the functional labels that often prevent NetWork.

THE EMERGENCE OF NETWORK

Corporations and organizations spend more than $35 billion annually to train, improve, and change people, but most of their investment returns little to the bottom line. The typical training and development program flits from one change effort to another in a vain attempt to modify people's behaviors to accommodate the latest "flavor of the month" fad. This approach never fully taps the power of human potential because it deals only with powerful work and, consequently, drives people into the excessive activity syndrome (stressing busyness over productiveness), as they continually respond to and conform to another person's or organization's agendas, but never find the essence of their own individual worth or maximize their own unique contributions.

To make matters worse, when responding to today's daunting challenges and opportunities, many managers just keep turning up the heat on their employees, who soon reach the breaking point. *Time* magazine, in a recent cover story, reported a common lament among today's workers: "Technology is increasing the heartbeat. We are inundated with information. The mind can't handle it all. The pace is so fast now, I sometimes feel like a gunfighter dodging bullets." People can't possibly think for themselves, evaluate their lives, consider their organization's values, find better paths, or live their lives the way they want if they're constantly dodging bullets.

In a values survey conducted by consulting and training firm Priority Management, *The Values Gap: An International Survey of Time and Value Conflicts in the 1990s Workplace,* the authors surveyed 1,000 middle- and upper-management professionals from Australia, Belgium, Canada, Ireland, New Zealand, Portugal, Singapore, Spain, the United Kingdom, and the United States. In the introduction to the survey results, the authors write:

> The new economy has resulted in the globalization of markets, increased competition and an accelerated pace of change, all driven by new and more flexible technologies. The result is heightened pressure at work to increase productivity, quality, variety and convenience, and to do it all in record time. This survey highlights the realities of living and working in the new economy, and, in particular, the widening gap between what we hope to achieve in a work day as opposed to the reality of what we actually do. . . . *We believe that many of the benefits of future economic development will accrue to those individuals, companies and nations who realize the integral role personal values play in shaping the work perspective.* When we're far-sighted, we seek to balance personal and corporate values in the workplace in order to reap benefits in both our personal and professional lives. (italics are author's emphasis)

There is a growing need for more NetWork, which develops and marshals people in concert with financial and physical resources to produce superior results. Unfortunately, such studies offer little in the way of solutions, except "work at it." Real solutions will, we think, require replacing current organizational change philosophies with the idea of NetWork.

NetWorking can help management move in the right direction by engaging in more dialogue with existing and prospective employees about talents, preferences, motivations, attitudes, and beliefs. At the same time, job hunters should closely examine an organization's commitment to fostering talent, facilitating common purpose, encouraging personal growth, and structuring teams before they join the organization. Individuals must go well beyond matching personal values with organizational values to forge an intimate and deep relationship between the individual and the organization based on genuine common purposes. For the best-run organizations in the new economy, that goal has already become a top management priority. However, NetWorking alone cannot meet all of an organization's performance challenges.

THE THIRD DIMENSION:
DISCOVERING VALUEWORK

In the early 1980s, Logan, Utah, looked like many other rural towns, as it steadily lost its business base and suffered a rising unemployment rate. Based on a traditional agricultural economy in the surrounding Cache Valley area, this small college town of 30,000 people experienced all the travails associated with an economy in transition. Actually, the community possessed many assets: a local university, budding centers of high-technology businesses, and a pioneering work ethic. However, Logan's efforts to promote local economic development had all but come to a standstill because city officials had failed to adopt a coordinated program. No one, it seemed, knew precisely what to do, and they all disagreed among themselves on what steps to take next.

Enter Bobbie Coray, a politically active housewife viewed by most of her neighbors as a woman who could get things done. Appointed as the region's first economic development director, she accepted the challenge to improve the local economy. Within her first week on the job, Coray understood the enormity of the task. No one called, not one business expressed interest in locating to the area, even the state offices of economic development failed to help. When finally asked by a visiting businessman for some information on the business climate of the region, Coray sheepishly admitted that she didn't have any. That's when she went to work, organizing written materials, bartering with local printers for price discounts, and borrowing the expertise of advertising students at the local university in order to fashion an inviting image for the community. She became a "stowaway" on recruiting trips that the state funded, and she piggy-backed on business trips local businesspeople made to cities in California. To streamline responses to requests for information, she automated a database to track all available information about each lead, and she developed proposal frameworks that allowed her to drop in information and customize materials that went to interested businesses within one day of their phone call. By performing PowerWork, she increased results with a severely limited staff.

However, it quickly became apparent that she needed to do more. Intuitively recognizing that a regional economic development strategy must not only spell out objectives but build a common vision, she formed a team of community leaders and outside professional facilitators to forge a comprehensive strategy and common vision for the economic development of the area. Eventually, she applied the skills of 150 community leaders to complex problems she herself could not solve. Private engineers donated their time, environmentalists and land developers worked side by side, and businesses contributed health care experts and funded professional strategists, all in an effort to increase the community's economic development competence. As these individuals worked together, the forged alliances and relationships that fostered a growing common purpose among Logan and Cache Valley citizens. NetWorking was taking place.

Since becoming a site for new businesses meant competing with other communities, Coray convinced Cache Valley community leaders that they needed to discover new insights into what their community, and no other, could offer. The team of community leaders and involved citizens embarked on an intensive discovery program aimed at pinpointing what unique value they could create for the benefit of all Logan and Cache Valley businesses and citizens.

The discovery program resulted in an interesting conclusion: Emerging businesses require a protective and secluded environment in which to grow, one removed from the scrutiny of Wall Street and outside competition. In such an environment, highly technical new businesses could enjoy the time and privacy needed to nurture and grow new concepts. How, the team wondered, could Logan and Cache Valley do a better job of creating such a business incubation environment than any other in the state or region? It would take an unprecedented united effort and a clear focus, they concluded, but it could be done.

Eventually their efforts paid off and the business incubation environment became the key promotional point in all of the community's advertising, as well as the focus of the community's economic development strategy to produce the greatest value for the greatest number of businesses and citizens. Ultimately, discovering valuable work paid off handsomely. In the four years since Logan's intensive economic development effort, the economy of Logan and the surrounding Cache Valley area has grown ever stronger. Unemployment in Cache County dropped from one of the highest to the lowest in the state. Selective job and tax base growth, without sacrificing quality of life, made the area the envy of its neighbors, and the Logan and Cache Valley economic development strategy development process has become a model for numerous communities throughout the western United States. Bobbie Coray herself has won a lot of recognition and awards and finds herself in constant demand as a speaker. Wherever her future leads her, Bobbie Coray will take with her the ability to work in all three dimensions: doing PowerWork, developing NetWork, and discovering ValueWork.

THE ESSENCE OF VALUEWORK

Think of ValueWork as "making innovative breakthroughs" or "climbing to new heights." ValueWork involves discovering useful knowledge and applying it to produce greater value (something of more worth, benefit, or importance than what is currently available) for more people.

- ValueWorkers are motivated by discovering new ideas and inventions that generate far-reaching influence throughout the world.

- They exhibit attributes such as knowledge lust, exhaustive searching, logical and lateral thinking, and breakthrough creation.

- People who excel at ValueWorking are best identified by their superior ability to organize ideas, improve the quality of life, and maximize progress.

- The ValueWorker's secret to improvement lies in continuously satisfying, exceeding, and pioneering customer needs. They constantly ask, "What should I discover now?"

No matter how effectively or efficiently you work every day on the job, and no matter how well you sharpen your talents and integrate your efforts with other people, if you do not discover new ways to add more value for the benefit of more people, you have not really done ValueWork.

Paul Allen, the man who cofounded Microsoft with Bill Gates in the mid-1970s, has been investing his billions in what he considers the most valuable arena of work in the future—the I-way (information highway). According to Allen, the most valuable work he can discover lies in marrying video technology, computer technology, and networking, whose convergence makes up the emerging information highway. To achieve this result, he began by asking questions such as: "What can we do that people haven't thought about in their individual areas?" "What wholly new applications, interfaces, products, and services can we deliver?" These sorts of questions had originally preoccupied Allen and Gates when they founded Microsoft, and they have led Allen to invest almost $1 billion in 20 companies that are discovering valuable work at key points along the information highway. His investments include Asymetrix, a software building tools developer; Starwave, a sports on-line service; ARI Network Services, an I-net commercial order taker and bill collector; Cardinal Technologies, a PC sound card manufacturer; Lone Wolf, a networker of all manner of electronic devices; Dream Works, the Spielberg-Katzenbach-Geffen motion picture studio; Paul Allen Group, a tightly knit collection of companies that trade ideas and do deals; Metricom, a developer of inexpensive wireless data connections for PCs; Surefind, a multimedia database navigating system developer; and Virtual Vision, a manufacturer of eyeglasses with a built-in screen. Clearly, Paul Allen has devoted himself—body, mind, and soul—to discovering valuable work.

Whenever visionary innovators like Paul Allen have produced greater value for a greater number of people, they have invariably made a huge contribution. Oddly, however, even in today's advanced society, most people still ascribe spectacular individual or organizational success to "luck," "fortune," "fate," "being at the right place at the right time," or "good karma." Worse, even the best contemporary minds fall into the trap of explaining success as just doing more PowerWork than everyone else. Once in a while, someone stresses the importance of NetWork but then attributes the success to "stumbling upon" or "unexpectedly discovering" an unknown talent or strength. Even more rarely does the idea of searching for and discovering ValueWork inform a description of success. At the heart of this dilemma lies the reality that ValueWork always resists easy identification and quantification. You can so much more easily see the evidence of the first dimension or the second dimension of work at play. In reality, however, the most successful people perform in all three dimensions.

THE SEARCH FOR VALUEWORK

When Henry Ford mass-produced the first automobiles, he gained enormous influence and rewards as he set out to deliver better transportation for everyone. The Ford Motor Company created and delivered great value to a mass market based on one man's commitment to valuable work. Tom Watson inaugurated IBM's commitment to customer service by emphasizing rental or leasing of its machines, sorters, tabulators, time clocks, and typewriters. Watson knew that his salespeople would develop a totally different attitude toward customers if the company retained ownership of the equipment. This self-enforced guarantee that IBM would always take care of its customers not only gave customers what they wanted, but turned IBM into the most productive customer service operation in the world. Again, one man's commitment to produce a greater value for a greater number drove a great corporation to amazing heights.

Unfortunately, in the early 1990s, IBM began delivering less and less value to fewer and fewer customers when it failed to capitalize on the technological and business trends that created the personal computer industry, holding on too long to Tom Watson's original formula, and eventually falling behind such rivals as Apple Computer, Compaq, and Hewlett-Packard. IBM's recent difficulties underscore the need for an ever-vigilant emphasis on all three dimensions of work.

ValueWork affects all aspects of life from the most personal quest to society's greatest challenges. In his epic work, *The Discoverers,* Daniel Boorstin, well-known historian and Pulitzer Prize winner, reveals the history of ValueWork: Each new generation finds or creates new knowledge that eventually gets supplanted by the next wave of new knowledge. Although anyone can discover ValueWork, relatively few people throughout history have focused unflaggingly on it, partially because discovering ValueWork tests individuals and organizations like no other endeavor. It's all too easy to fall prey to illusions. The "illusions of knowledge," developed by one set of discoverers, inevitably become obstacles to discovery for those who follow. The discoveries of Ptolemy, Herodotus, Petrarch, Socrates, Galileo, Columbus, Marco Polo, Newton, Paracelsus, Darwin, Freud, Marx, and Einstein produced great value for a great number, but then, a subsequent discoverer produced even greater value for a greater number, a historical fact that illuminates a timeless truth: *The greatest progress stems from constant discovery.* Those who continue to provide the greatest value for the greatest number in their chosen work will consistently win in the long run.

Regardless of your specific realms of endeavor, your personal or organizational results will always remain limited unless you work each and every day in all three dimensions: doing Power-Work, developing NetWork, and discovering ValueWork. MetaWork ties it all together and thus helps individuals, teams, and entire organizations accomplish more than they ever imagined possible.

THE FOURTH DIMENSION: DETERMINING METAWORK

MetaWork for individuals requires moving outside your comfort zone. MetaWork for teams involves combining natural Power-Workers with natural NetWorkers and ValueWorkers, and MetaWork for organizations means orchestrating the full range of human potential to meet short- and long-term objectives. By tying together all dimensions, individuals, teams, and organizations move into the fourth dimension where they can achieve amazing results.

Building up her medical practice in a suburb of Cincinnati, Ohio, Dr. Levy constantly strives for efficiency in her work. She genuinely seeks to provide quality medical care, while reducing the burden of health care costs for her patients. Every day she asks herself, "How can I do my work faster, better, or cheaper?" Together with her staff of three nurses, a receptionist, and an office manager, Dr. Levy strives to increase the number of patients she sees during a day without compromising the quality of health care. Her team develops office routines to ensure that every necessary thing gets done right, making it possible for patients to move quickly and efficiently through standardized procedures that begin with the receptionist, who introduces the patient into the system; continue with the nurses, who gather information and take samples; move to Dr. Levy herself, who diagnoses and prescribes treatment; and end with the office manager, who handles billing and insurance. The team reviews office routines monthly and makes necessary changes to improve efficiency.

On the next level, Dr. Levy begins to question her effectiveness, asking herself, "How can I eliminate or reduce the amount of unnecessary work that I'm doing while increasing or adding more of the important work?" She still spends too much time performing tasks other than diagnosis, her most important function, and she still doesn't receive complete information (i.e., results for lab tests) before meeting with patients. To solve these problems, she and her staff redesigned the work flow to maximize her diagnosis time and eliminate premature and unnecessary patient discussions. Unlike most doctor's offices, where 90 percent of the patient's time is spent leafing through *People* magazine, patients can now come to the office any time, without an appointment, during extended office hours, to provide samples, take tests, give information, and schedule a meeting with the physician for the following day, after she has received the test results. The reengineered work system increases the physician's diagnosis time, minimizes duplication of effort between her and her nurses, eliminates unnecessary or premature patient visits, improves patient satisfaction, allows for emergency visits, and increases demand for her services. Dr. Levy and her staff have now increased their productivity by adding effective work to efficient work. In short, their work has become more powerful.

Dr. Levy could have stopped here, as many do, but instead she resolves to become even more productive by further developing her skills and nurturing relationships for increased advantage and competence compared to other family practice physicians in the Cincinnati area. She asks herself, "How can I better apply and develop my skills and form relationships for the increased advantage of my practice and patients?" After conducting an in-depth review of her medical practice, she realizes that her long-standing commitment to and study of illness prevention and wellness programs distinguishes her from other doctors in the area. She also recognizes that she has always gained her greatest fulfillment as a physician from diagnosing a patient's general health and prescribing a personalized wellness program. Not until now does she so clearly understand that her natural interest and developed strength in preventative medicine have created an important advantage for her practice on which she can and should build. As she and her staff focus their practice on wellness, they enhance their reputation with a growing number of patients from surrounding communities who desire wellness assistance. Over time, Dr. Levy extends her practice, adding nurses and physicians to meet the rapidly increasing demand for her services. She has now added NetWork to PowerWork, continuously striving to remain productive in both dimensions.

Although she has achieved great success in her medical career and has benefited thousands of patients, Dr. Levy believes she can become even more productive by discovering new and better ways to do more good for more people. Achieving even greater productivity may take years to accomplish, but she begins by asking herself, "How can I create more valuable health care benefits for more patients?" This question spurs her to expand the boundaries of her thinking to patients outside the reach of her practice area. She contemplates several options: opening offices and clinics in Columbus, Cleveland, Toledo, and Detroit; providing training to interested physicians around the country; retiring from practice to teach at a medical school; writing a book on her insights into wellness and preventative medicine; consulting with health care providers to establish better wellness programs; and so on. Finally, after considerable time and effort, she discovers that patients vastly prefer personalized wellness guidelines to more general ones. To incorporate this new finding into her work, she forms TotalHealth, Inc., to develop two CD-ROM, multimedia software programs for national distribution. The first offers a medically sophisticated program, based on data from lab tests, for physicians to use in diagnosing their patients' general health, with the goal of prescribing a personalized prevention and wellness regimen. The second provides another less technical program for consumers, based on medical history, diagnosed conditions, lifestyle habits, height, weight, age, gender, occupation, and psychological type. After their market introduction, the two TotalHealth programs quickly become best-sellers, creating greater value for a greater number of people. Dr. Levy now uses her expanded financial resources to open clinics around the United States, introduce updated wellness software programs, and teach medical school classes by satellite; all her efforts are aimed at helping more and more people live healthier lives. By adding ValueWork to NetWork and PowerWork, Dr. Levy has maximized her overall productivity, producing more success and fulfillment for herself, as well as more health and well-being for others. Much larger organizations can follow the same path.

With this broad overview of MetaWork's three dimensions in mind, let's probe more deeply into how you, similar to Dr. Levy, can improve your work in all three. Chapters 2–4 explore one of MetaWork's dimensions and show exactly how you can become a PowerWorker, a NetWorker, and a ValueWorker.

CHAPTER TWO

PowerWorkers

"There are risks and costs to a programme of action.
But they are far less than the long-range risks and costs of
comfortable inaction."

John F. Kennedy

A DAY IN THE LIFE OF A POWERWORKER

At precisely 6:00 A.M., advertising executive JoAnn Lynch (a
fictional character) wakes up her six-year-old twins, Stacey and
Scott, for school. Although JoAnn has been following a well-
established schedule for months, she always encounters surprises that force her to alter the routine. Recently, she added a
15-minute buffer to the schedule after Scott poured a jar of
honey on Stacey's hair, making everyone late for the day's activities. Today, however, the twins get up immediately, make their
beds, dress themselves, join their Dad for a bowl of cereal with
fruit, then quietly wait for Mom to take them to school. They
know this is Mom's "no nonsense" time.

JoAnn has been up since 4:30 A.M., finalizing a presentation
she will make to a prospective client during a lunch meeting
today. At 6:45 A.M., she kisses her husband Ted good-bye, loads
her twins into the Land Rover, and drops them off at the private
school near their home.

"Be smart. Work hard. I love you," she says.

"Bye, Mommy. I love you."

"Me, too."

"Mary will take you to the mall tonight. Dad and I will meet you there. Bye."

JoAnn waves good-bye.

JoAnn arrives at her office before 7:30 A.M. and reviews her schedule for the day, filling in any vacant spaces on her day planner.

JoAnn is a 37-year-old vice president and senior account executive with Newhouse-Dunne, Ltd., a midsize Chicago-based advertising agency with $50 million in annual revenues and 116 employees. Her 10th-floor office overlooks Lake Michigan at 900 Michigan Avenue. A day planner lies on her well-organized desk, open to Thursday, March 29th, and it reveals a packed day:

7:45 A.M.	Deliver final changes on DigiCom proposal to Graphics.
8:00 A.M.	Meet with Williams and Stoffel on Motorola project.
8:30 A.M.	Call Ray Ivie to set meeting time. Check with Jack on Baxter proposal. Call Susan Black at 8:50 on her car phone.
9:00 A.M.	Creative design session—Sara Lee
10:00 A.M.	Final review of DigiCom presentation
10:30 A.M.	Reorganize account files with Kelly—match with computer files.
11:30 A.M.	Final dress rehearsal with DigiCom presentation team
12:00 Noon	DigiCom lunch meeting—University Club
2:00 P.M.	Develop budget for new FMC brochure.
2:30 P.M.	Review March statements—change Unicom and Abbott.

2:55 P.M.   Call Mary—Scott & Stacey's dentist appointment.

3:00 P.M.   Client approval meeting—Walgreen's Annual report lay-out and preliminary design

4:00 P.M.   Return calls.
                 Follow-up with WGN on Perry Homes press release.
                 Call prime contact list.
                 Check with Market Surveillance for leads.
                 Call Ted.

4:30 P.M.   Conference call with ServiceMaster Customer focus network—make sure Nichols joins in.

5:00 P.M.   Review customer survey results—Cotter & Blaisdell.

5:30 P.M.   Task force meeting—revamp billing procedures.

7:00 P.M.   Meet Ted and kids at the mall.

10:00 P.M.   Review Friday's schedule.

Thursday flies by with few hitches, and about 8:30 P.M. that night, while Scott and Stacey ride the mall's "Rolling Waves" kiddie rollercoaster for the fifth time, JoAnn and Ted share a brief moment of semiprivacy.

"So, how was your day," inquires Ted.

"The usual frenzy."

"Mine, too. Six depositions, three court filings, and a ridiculous staff meeting." Ted works for a large corporate law firm downtown.

"Thank goodness, it's Thursday."

"Ted smiles. "Why's that?"

"One day closer to a glorious weekend!"

"What did you have in mind?" asks Ted as he gently draws JoAnn into an embrace.

Just then, Scott and Stacey run up, finally weary of the "Rolling Wave" ride. JoAnn and Ted clasp hands, each dreaming of a quiet weekend with the kids.

A model PowerWorker, JoAnn Lynch packs her days with productive work. Far from living a stress-filled life, she allocates her time wisely, making every minute count. She follows this simple rule:

THE POWERWORKER'S CREDO

I am activity conscious, performance driven, and results oriented. I bring discipline and realism to my work, always striving to strengthen and protect all the situations in which I participate.

Adhering to this credo enables the PowerWorker to produce results, but taken to the extreme, it can trap a person in a web of excessive "busyness" that can narrow one's perspective about work and life, squeezing out creative thinking, diminishing learning and growth, and harming relationships. While working to master this dimension of work, you should not let it preoccupy your life to the point where it prohibits you from moving into the other dimensions, NetWorking and ValueWorking. In the pages ahead, we explore this First Dimension of work more thoroughly in an attempt to help you harness its power in your own endeavors.

POWERWORKING

In the early 1980s, many consultants, executives, and academics left their employment to form new consulting businesses, exploiting a window of opportunity that had opened for those eager to improve organizations with the new tools of organizational redesign. The idea gained great popularity in the early 1990s with the success of the title, *Reengineering the Corporation,* but a number of business thinkers were offering whole-system design programs long before Hammer and Champy published their book in 1993.

Corporate growth during the 1980s had so greatly strained the traditional structures of most organizations that it didn't take long for their executives to begin searching for a better way. To aid them in their search, the new breed of consultants developed a method of organizational redesign that analyzed an organization's processes such as planning, information, accounting, purchasing, and then refocused them on the main needs of the customer and the fundamental objectives of the business. Although they could clearly see the benefits of this methodology, and even though executives were questioning the viability of conventional arrangements, these "pioneers" ran into a lot of resistance early on because the concept of redesigning all of an organization's processes struck most people as extreme and even dangerous. As Starr Eckholdt recalls, "Early on, my clients weren't those companies that really needed my service. Instead, the most interested companies were those at the forefront of their industries. They were constantly looking ahead and always asking themselves, 'How do we stay in the lead?' They included companies such as Corning Glass, UNUM Life Insurance, Washington Water & Power, and others that eventually pioneered the ideas we now call reengineering."

Quite naturally, the success of reengineering has also attracted a host of competitors. "In the beginning there were only a couple of firms doing what I'm doing," Eckholdt says. "Now it seems that every consulting group from the largest to the smallest has become a reengineering specialist." Today, all of the Big 6 accounting-consulting firms offer reengineering services to their clients, and powerhouses such as Booz Allen, McKinsey & Company, Boston Consulting Group, and EDS have also moved into the field. Many center their redesign programs around technology and information management, a trend Eckholdt finds severely limiting because it overemphasizes technology at the expense of the true benefits of reengineering, namely, making a whole organization more effective and efficient at getting results.

One of Starr's clients (we refer to the company as Webco to protect its privacy), a midsize national insurance company, embraced Eckholdt's broader view. Webco, fully committed to getting better, faster, and more cost-effective results, virtually shut down one large division for two weeks of intense reengineering. In the words of President and CEO Tom Chamberlain (not his real name), "We brought everyone to Sawgrass Resort near Jacksonville, Florida, for a week to reengineer everything in the division's business. After dramatically changing several work processes during the session, we implemented over 40 ideas of the hundreds proposed in the next 60 days. One idea will save the company around $6 million a year."

Webco kept its focus on greater effectiveness and efficiency by acknowledging reality, no matter how painful. "The hardest part was facing up to reality," says Chamberlain. "No one deals with reality when they're in trouble, but that's where reengineering begins. You have to ask tough questions: Do we have the right people? Do we have the right systems? Do we have the right resources? It's painful because you often let people go, close down operations, or push the organization outside its comfort zone. We know reengineering isn't a panacea. It cannot guarantee success, but it represents our commitment to getting dramatically better results all the time."

Webco's reengineering effort required wholehearted commitment, observes Liz Fairchild, VP of Human Resources: "It was an intense effort to improve every employee's knowledge of our products, procedures, processes, and services. We completely shut down our revenue stream, stopped doing what we normally do, and spent one week examining all our products, services, and processes. We made a company commitment to find out how we can best serve our customers. As a result, our people are more responsive, energetic, and dedicated. We feel that we're providing better products and services to our customers than ever before. But this is just a beginning, not an ending."

As the Webco example demonstrates, an emphasis on true PowerWork can enable a company to focus on the right things to do, then to do them right.

THE BASICS OF POWERWORK

A mechanic picks the right tool for the right job. Instead of the old army slogan, "If you can't fix it with a hammer or a coat of paint, get rid of it," the skilled mechanic says, "I can fix anything with the right tools." Good managers think that way, too. Rather than trying to turn a singles batter into a slugger, Casey Stengal would recruit the most talented player for the cleanup spot, and, as he once said, a manager's "ability is the art of getting credit for all the home runs someone else hits." From Indianapolis 500 race car drivers to major league baseball managers and frontline workers, PowerWorkers always stand out because they know how to get the job done. Mario Andretti, Leo Durocher, Lyle Anderson, Yogi Berra, and the guy who keeps a battered old Plymouth purring like a cat are all Power-Workers who share an innate ability to produce results.

PowerWork is like thinning beets at the farm. As you look down the long rows, you wonder if you will ever reach the end. However, even though the task is repetitive and feels as though it will take forever, if you put your head down and focus on the space between the last beet you left in the ground and the next, you'll eventually get to the end of the row. At its very roots, PowerWork involves a few basics:

- The key objective of PowerWork
- The common activities of PowerWorkers
- The required knowledge for PowerWorking
- The natural bias in PowerWork

Let's take a closer look at each of these fundamentals.

---

1. THE KEY OBJECTIVE OF POWERWORK

♦ PowerWork focuses on the key objective of doing work that leads directly, without deviations, to producing more for less.

♦ Two simple questions can help you focus your attention daily on the key objective of PowerWork:

• What work will achieve the right results?
• What work will distract us from achieving the right results?

♦ You can always recognize a PowerWorking objective by its focus on practical, concrete, and measurable results.

♦ PowerWorking objectives help you choose, from the wide range of possible tasks each day, the work most crucial and essential to accomplishing the targeted results.

In the early 1980s, Apple Computer created a unique computer operating system that demystified the confusing language of computer programmers and simplified the use of the machine. With its innovative mouse, even a child could direct the personal computer (PC), and with its friendly desktop screen, a whole new generation of users flocked into the PC Age. Apple did not just happen onto its discoveries by accident. The company carefully created its technology to address the needs of computer users in a way that could overcome their natural resistance to complex programming or operating languages. Propelled by this user vision, Apple computers began to achieve a preeminent position in the marketplace.

Despite its vision, however, Apple repeatedly failed at PowerWorking by underemphasizing practical results, restricting the use of its new operating system to its own hardware, and ultimately failing to fully exploit its innovations.

Today, Apple wrestles with increasing competition, especially from Microsoft with its Windows operating system, which now dominates the marketplace because of its applicability across a variety of PC platforms to a broader range of users. Although Windows remains slightly inferior to Apple's Macintosh operating system, it has succeeded in producing the right results at the right time. Apple lost the momentum of opportunity when it failed to apply its original discovery to the larger PC market. Had it done so, perhaps more people would be buying Macintosh software instead of Windows software today.

2. THE COMMON ACTIVITIES OF POWERWORKERS

♦ Powerworkers are great *organizers* and *maximizers* who get the most from the least by establishing dynamic structures and systems that emphasize right work and discourage wrong work (waste and inefficiency).

♦ You can keep your organizing and maximizing skills in peak condition by continuously

  • Finding better, faster, or more cost-effective ways to organize your work.
  • Increasing the amount of right work you perform.

- Eliminating more wrong work (work that wastes time, energy, and resources because it does not produce the right results).

◆ You can identify Powerworkers in their organizing or maximizing modes when they closely examine their organizations, evaluating every work activity, looking for areas of duplication, identifying nonessential activities, and pushing the work system to its natural limits.

◆ Effective organizing and maximizing build power because such efforts result in doing better, faster, and more cost-effective work.

Rebecca Matthias could not find the right sort of stylish maternity clothes to wear for work. Believing that many other women shared her frustration, she started a company, Mothers Work, whose annual sales have grown to $56 million in a decade, and which expects to become a billion-dollar powerhouse in the next. Matthias not only figured out that "right work" in the women's clothing industry meant manufacturing a wide variety of stylish maternity clothes, but she also learned the importance of doing work faster than competitors. With the help of her husband, the company developed a computer system called Trendtrack, which it uses to monitor sales in more than 100 company-owned stores across the United States. Trendtrack makes it possible to track sales by the moment, order items immediately from the warehouse, restock warehouses quickly, minimize outlet storage space, and eliminate unnecessary administrative work. It also makes the company's manufacturing and ordering system the fastest in the industry, an achievement that produces a lot of satisfied customers. Matthias, too, is a Power-Worker, who has learned to maximize her own effectiveness, and that of her company, by doing more right things, and by doing those things well.

3. THE REQUIRED KNOWLEDGE FOR POWERWORKING

♦ PowerWorking depends on understanding the realities of the business circumstances, the cost structure, available resources, operating constraints, inputs, and outputs.

♦ You can remain knowledgeable about Powerwork by continuously asking one question: Is it time to totally rethink our costs and resources?

♦ You know you are gaining knowledge for PowerWorking when you immerse yourself in the concrete facts and details surrounding a business situation.

♦ Effective Powerworking enables you to strike the optimum balance between doing right work and doing it at the least possible cost with the most appropriate resouces.

Margaret Thompson and Brenda Reiss-Brennan, owners and managers of Family Health Outcomes, a small mental health clinic, had just concluded a presentation to a disinterested human resources director. Thompson and Reiss-Brennan had offered a proposal to provide the prospective client company with mental healthcare services for all of its employees, and they had heard an all-too-typical response from the human resources director: "I know that the productivity of our workers is affected by their mental health, but I have no idea which approaches work and which don't. I can't bet the company's money on your program because I have so many unresolved questions about it. I've got to watch over health coverage costs so they don't get out of hand."

In the past, most employers have avoided coming to grips with mental health coverage, and neither they nor insurance companies have been able to agree on what approach really works. Given the increasing pressures nationwide to reduce healthcare costs, the dilemma has only worsened. Thompson and Reiss-Brennan knew this all too well, so they went back to their office in a rather somber mood. "The problem with our industry," said Thompson, "is that most of us don't look at what we do as a business. None of our therapists worry about the costs they incur or the resources they use in their work. Even worse, therapists can't quantify or precisely identify the benefits of their services. We seem to get so caught up with helping our clients that we forget to consider the cost effectiveness or actual benefits of our product."

Reiss-Brennan agreed and added, "There's no common methodology to guide how they [therapists] should treat patients. Therapists do what they think best, all the time knowing in the back of their minds that insurance coverage is limited. Their fear that the coverage will run out before the patient has improved always gets in the way."

Over the next few months, the two partners decided to change their approach, making it more sensitive to the resource constraints of employers and more oriented to real patient improvement. Their years of experience had taught them that if a patient's mental illness receives early treatment, it is less likely to escalate into a more serious problem. However, early or preventative treatment means packing in more visits up front in a condensed time period. It also means incurring a greater initial cost, eating more of the insurance coverage early on, and leaving little for ongoing treatment and monitoring. The more Thompson and Reiss-Brennan designed a new approach, the more it seemed to contradict reason. Reiss-Brennan captured the issue succinctly: "With limited financial resources, why spend more early on and risk losing a patient before the end of treatment?"

As the two healthcare entrepreneurs wrestled with the dilemma, they gradually hammered out a revised approach. A key element would be a seminar for employees on how to prevent stress, anxiety, and depression. In this seminar, employees would receive newly designed self-assessment tools that they could apply on their own. Anyone who determined a need for counseling could then make a confidential request for treatment, which Thompson and Reiss-Brennan expanded to include the families of the patient. If the families got involved in the treatment, they reasoned, the patients stood a much better chance of overcoming a mental health problem.

Their first presentations of this new product to prospective customers proved difficult because the revised approach appeared more costly, especially in light of the fact that many of the costs now occurred up front. However, Thompson and Reiss-Brennan assured potential customers that these up-front costs would be more than offset by more effective treatment that would end sooner and cost less in the long run. They also promised fewer mental health problems among the client's employees over time.

According to Reiss-Brennan, "We weren't positive at first how well this approach would turn out, not only from the standpoint of controlling costs, but also in terms of providing successful treatment to patients. We hoped for the best."

Her hopes have proved to be well founded, as slowly but surely, customers are responding to the new approach and are beginning to experience reduced incidents of mental breakdown or illness after a year on the program. Demand for their services continues to increase.

In retrospect, Thompson observes, "When we began considering ways to better manage scarce resources and to maximize results, it changed our whole way of thinking. We had never used the term 'bottom line' in our office before. Now we not only scrutinize our own bottom line in detail, we have been able to show that our approach can help our customers strengthen their 'bottom line' by improving the well-being of their employees and thus reducing overall mental health costs."

4. THE NATURAL BIAS IN POWERWORK

♦ Above all else, PowerWorkers are *doers.*

♦ To increase your ability to perform PowerWork, you should

  • Pay attention to details.

- Be here now (that means focus on your present circumstances).
- Keep the "line of sight" to right results, clear and unobstructed.

♦ You can always recognize natural PowerWorkers by their strong bias toward "getting things done." They often rise to the top of their organizations.

♦ Developing more of a bias toward "doing" involves seizing every opportunity to take action, wisely, of course.

Carl Jung, a chief founder of modern psychiatry, reminds us in his book, *Modern Man in Search of a Soul*, "The nearer we approach to the middle of life, and the better we have succeeded in entrenching ourselves in our personal standpoints and social positions, the more it appears as if we had discovered the right course and the right ideals and principles of behavior. For this reason we suppose them to be eternally valid, and make a virtue of unchangeably clinging to them." Change does not come easily for most people. Change if you can, but if you can't, try, at the very least, to understand and align yourself with PowerWorkers. Their effectiveness and efficiency may well rub off on you, but even if that doesn't happen, they will add immeasurable strength to your team or organization.

Some people are natural PowerWorkers, possessing an innate sense for getting results; organizing and maximizing performance; and paying attention to costs, resources, and constraints. Born doers, they relish the PowerWork dimension of work because they're good at it. This dimension of work makes sense to them. Natural PowerWorkers, regardless of their motivation, focus first and foremost on doing, acting, and making something happen. Whether they are free and independent entrepreneurs or bound and obligated bureaucrats, natural PowerWorkers grasp reality and deal with it decisively. Their realism serves them well when it comes to measuring performance, benchmark-ing best practices, or reengineering work processes, because they see details so clearly. Close associates often describe Power-Workers as organizational peak performers, pillars of the com-munity, backbones of society, or simply the people who "get things done." Doing PowerWork comes naturally and easily to them.

However, not all natural PowerWorkers exhibit superior talent for PowerWorking, and not everyone possesses an instinct for PowerWorking in the first place. If you consider yourself a natural PowerWorker with underdeveloped capabilities, you can gain steady ground with a self-improvement program such as the one outlined later in this chapter. Because this dimension of work is comfortable to you, you can quite easily improve your effectiveness and efficiency.

People who do not consider themselves to be natural Power-Workers may want to study this chapter more carefully. Any-one can become a better PowerWorker, whether that person enjoys natural gifts in this dimension or not. Likewise, simply understanding the PowerWork dimension can benefit you in team and organizational settings where you may find yourself relying more heavily on the contribution of natural Power-Workers.

You can reap the benefits of PowerWorking by first assess-ing, then improving your own effectiveness and efficiency.

ASSESSING POWERWORK

Many children provide a classic example of beginning Power-Work. They will usually clean their rooms only to the expecta-tion level of their parents, expending the least amount of effort necessary before being allowed to play. If you look behind the drawers or under the bed, and particularly, if you examine something not previously on the inspection tour, you will proba-bly find out how they have been cleaning their rooms so fast.

Workers cannot set about improving their effectiveness and efficiency without first assessing the present levels and expectations for their work. Conduct this PowerWork evaluation by answering the following questions for yourself, your team, and/ or your organization (Fig. 2.1). A score between 45 and 60 gives you outstanding marks in PowerWorking; scores between 30 and 44 show a need for continuous improvement; any score

Figure 2.1. PowerWork self-evaluation.

For the period beginning _____ , and ending _____ , answer the following questions by circling the number on the continuum that best describes your assessment of PowerWork during the period specified:

	Yes	Somewhat	No
1. Did you get better, faster, and cheaper results?	6 5 4	3 2	1 0
2. Did you do more "right work" and less "wrong work?"	6 5 4	3 2	1 0
3. Have you accomplished the tasks, priorities, and goals you planned?	6 5 4	3 2	1 0
4. Have you measured your performance?	6 5 4	3 2	1 0
5. Have you benchmarked your efforts with the "best in world" practices of others?	6 5 4	3 2	1 0
6. Did you redesign work processes to increase effectiveness and efficiency?	6 5 4	3 2	1 0
7. Did you exhibit a bias toward action, always adapting as necessary?	6 5 4	3 2	1 0
8. Did you improve your ability to organize work and maximize results?	6 5 4	3 2	1 0
9. Did you pay close attention to the cost structure and available resources as you worked?	6 5 4	3 2	1 0
10. Do you consider yourself a better PowerWorker now than you did at the beginning of this period?	6 5 4	3 2	1 0

between 15 and 29 means making some major changes; and a score of 14 or less indicates a need for substantial adjustment in your attitude toward your work.

The PowerWorkers you encounter in this chapter would all score quite high on this test, possibly even 60. Regardless of the score you award yourself, your team, or your organization, you can take certain immediate steps to improve or maintain it.

IMPROVING POWERWORK

If you scored high on the PowerWork self-evaluation, don't sit back and relax. A high score today does not guarantee a high score tomorrow. Constantly strive to maintain your high levels of effectiveness and efficiency. If you scored low, of course, you should embark on a program of improvement. In either case, you can maintain or improve your PowerWork by following three practical steps: measuring, benchmarking, and redesigning. Each step builds on the other, and, together, they encompass many of the current concepts that individuals, teams, and organizations are using to dramatically improve their competitiveness.

Step 1. Measuring: Identify and Measure Tasks That Will Produce the Right Results. When organizations encourage people to act as if they are operating their own businesses, the old adage, "If you can't measure it, you can't manage it," takes on new meaning. In order to achieve greater results in their work, everyone must recognize the resources at hand (i.e., time, materials, information, etc.) and measure the use of those resources in obtaining the desired results. One cannot gauge performance or gain the insight to take large independent strides to new levels of performance without the necessary measurements. To put this in perspective, just think about the impact of not keeping score during your golf game. Whether you're an amateur or professional golfer, if you never keep score, the pace of improvement in your competitiveness will fall behind those who do keep score and use that measurement to improve their game.

PowerWork always improves through measurement of performance. Proven business measurements such as financial ratios, market shares, sales increases, inventory turns, customer complaints, attitude surveys, MBOs, employee performance appraisals, productivity ratios, and "best in world" performance comparisons provide important indicators of where to begin taking action to improve performance.

Step 2. Benchmarking: Compare Your Work with Those Who Achieve Superior Results. The cliché "reinventing the wheel" has come to characterize inefficient and ineffective work. To avoid it, you can study and learn from the "best inventions" of others. That's really all that "benchmarking" means. Once you have identified and measured the components of your work, you can improve further by learning from those who have mastered these components better than anyone else. Successful benchmarking requires both an internal and external perspective, and while it usually leads to incremental improvement, it does keep you moving in the right direction toward greater effectiveness and efficiency. If you want to improve your tennis game, you'll learn a lot by watching how Pete Sampras serves, how Andre Agassi returns serves, or how Steffi Graf serves and rushes the net. No book can teach performance as well as a top performer can.

Identifying and implementing the best processes and practices of other individuals, teams, or organizations instills a spirit of continuous improvement such as no other single business activity does, because people always learn by watching others perform.

Step 3. Redesigning: Design New Methods of Performing Your Work That Will Substantially Enhance Your Ability to Achieve Greater Results. After measuring the components of your work and comparing them to "the best in class," you can position your operation for real innovation. This search for the new and revolutionary method entails the willingness to start from scratch and to question every assumption. It strives for a new process that delivers greater results, and it requires an external, customer-driven perspective. When Bill Walsh took over as head coach of the San Francisco 49ers, he redesigned the team's entire offensive approach, setting up the play-action passing game that made Joe Montana a superstar and racked up a series of Super Bowl championships. George Seifert and Steve Young now carry on the tradition of redesigning things when necessary.

At this advanced stage of PowerWorking, you should always look for the flaws or problems in existing work systems. All work processes function together as a whole system to satisfy customers. Success depends on breaking down functional boundaries and helping the entire organization understand how each process can add greater value for the customer.

Incorporating these three steps, U.S. West's *process management cycle* (Fig. 2.2) does one of two things with work processes: fix or redesign. U.S. West, headquartered in Denver, Colorado, is one of the original Baby Bells. The company established a common approach for monitoring work processes by applying the process management cycle to all of its business processes. U.S. West determines which processes the company can improve to consistently serve customers better: Fixing involves continuous improvement techniques that allow people to "do things differently." Other work processes, the ones the company can't fix through continuous improvement, undergo complete redesign as part of a total solution.

U.S. West's approach includes the three basic steps of measuring, benchmarking, and redesigning. In addition, it identifies and prioritizes improvement options. It all starts and ends with customer needs, and it provides for continuous examination of

Figure 2.2. U.S. West's process management cycle.

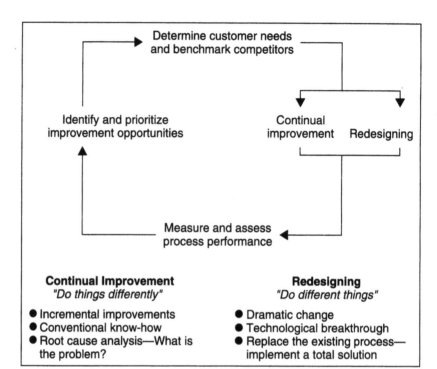

those needs and evaluation of how well the company is satisfying them. PowerWorkers do the same, constantly measuring, benchmarking, and redesigning their efforts to enhance effectiveness and efficiency.

At U.S. West, the results have proved the value of their approach. According to Duane Cook, a human resources manager at U.S. West, their process management cycle has led to a staff reduction of almost 10,000 employees. In his own words: "Some people ask, 'How can you improve service if you eliminate 10,000 jobs?'' The answer is that you don't do the same things the same way—you do different things and do things differently. We expect to become more efficient and provide better, faster service to customers. We don't have any choice."

ON BECOMING A POWERWORKER

At the wooing of a new group of investors, the ATK motorcycle company recently relocated to Utah after closing its plant in southern California where it had operated for eight years. A manufacturer of high-performance off-road motorcycles for a small market of enthusiasts across the country, ATK had grown out of the hobby interests of its new owner, Franklin White, who since his youth had ridden in motorcross races and "simply loved the sport."

Despite having won over a cult of devotees to the ATK bike, the company had suffered in recent years from poor design, high production costs, and intense foreign competition. ATK's prices had soared to the point where its product lay beyond most consumers' budgets. To maintain its high-end position, White knew that the company needed to improve the overall quality of its bike, and that doing so would require additional capital. Enter the new investors, who quickly infused it with two million dollars of sorely needed capital. In return, White promised quick results. Unfortunately, however, those results didn't materialize, as the company missed production deadlines and arguments broke out among the company's design team over new bike features. ATK dealers, finding it more and more difficult to sell the bikes, began dropping the product line from their showrooms. When pressed for cost information, White remained vague and inaccurate. Busily exploring hundreds of different ideas about improving his product, he failed to inspire action among the ranks.

The frustrated investors eventually removed White from the company presidency and installed Brad Angus in his place. Although Angus lacked motorcycle manufacturing experience, he had successfully overseen a number of production operations in other industries. He saw his first challenge clearly: engineering a complete and immediate change in attitude throughout the company. In his first meeting with the senior staff, Angus issued the challenge: "This company is on the edge. Unless we change what we are doing immediately, we do not deserve to stay, nor will we stay, in business."

Then he outlined exactly what he intended to do: Having reviewed the costs of the entire operation, he would immediately cut them by 50 percent. He then met with the design team and threw out three-fourths of their upcoming models, picking one moderately priced one to receive the bulk of everyone's attention. As he went on to question dealers and customers about what displeased them about ATK's product, he began addressing their concerns.

Although he began to win dealers and customers over, Angus heard from his critics, too. At a meeting of the board, one director argued, "Brad is moving too fast. He has only been there five days and he has already laid off half of the work force, changed the entire design of next year's products, and revamped the sales approach. I think he should take more time to think things through."

Angus didn't waffle. "This company has had the luxury of operating without feeling any pressure for results too long," he countered. "Most employees don't know how hard they need to work. They have lived in a world of dreams and ideas with no reality checks. Now, I'm forcing them to make decisions, take action, and implement improvements. If we're wrong, we'll change quickly until we get it right. But the inaction and dragging things out must stop. It's too dangerous."

Although ATK still faces many obstacles, it's moving in the right direction. Sales have risen, workers feel directed, and results have begun to materialize, all because Brad Angus brought a doer's mentality to the crisis.

LESSONS LEARNED

- ✔ PowerWorkers are doers, producers, and result-getters.
- ✔ PowerWork focuses primarily on getting results in the short term as the best way to keep getting results in the long term.

- ✔ Right work equals right results, and wrong work equals wrong results.

- ✔ PowerWorkers rely on organizing and maximizing skills to measure performance, benchmark progress, and redesign everything when necessary.

- ✔ Regardless of whether you are a natural PowerWorker or not, you can become better at PowerWorking by embracing all three levels of PowerWork: Measuring, Benchmarking, and Redesigning.

CHAPTER THREE

NetWorkers

"You can make more friends in two months by becoming interested in other people, than you can in two years by trying to get people interested in you."

Dale Carnegie

A DAY IN THE LIFE OF A NETWORKER

Trevor Corcoran (a fictional character) looks over to his night-stand to scan the red digitals of his clock radio—5:49 A.M. He rolls over to capture ten more minutes of sleep before he calls New York. After all, no one in New York City gets to the office before nine o'clock. At 6:10 A.M., Trevor places his call:

"Paine-Webber."

"Jack McNally, please."

"McNally speaking."

"Jack, it's Trevor."

"Trevor—I've been waiting for your call. I found what you wanted. We completed a full-blown market analysis of Bergen Brunsway last month, including a review of the Thompson division."

"How much can you share with me?"

"Whatever you want. It's public information, even though I'm doing you a big favor to let you see it early."

"Can you fax it to me?"

"Ninety pages?"

"Overnight it to me. Hang on a minute. My FedEx account number is 1926-5421."

For the next ten minutes, Trevor and Jack bring each other up to date on their business school classmates from Northwestern.

Between 6:30 A.M. and 7:00 A.M., Trevor makes five more calls to the East Coast, gathering and sharing information about the latest merger and acquisition rumors in the electronics industry.

From 7:00 A.M. to 8:30 A.M., Trevor showers, intermittently watches CNN and "The Today Show," drinks a glass of orange juice, and munches on an English muffin while scanning the *Wall Street Journal, The New York Times,* the *Chicago Tribune,* the *Dallas Herald,* the *San Francisco Chronicle,* the *Los Angeles Times,* and *Investor News Daily.*

After spending an hour talking with his wife, Candice, and playing with his four-year-old son, Chase, Trevor arrives at the San Francisco Art Center at 10:00 A.M. for an Arts Council board meeting. After the meeting, during the board luncheon, Trevor sits with Rod Caulfield, CFO of TransAmerica and Liz Winger, senior vice president of Wells Fargo Bank, sharing gossip about the latest mergers, joint-ventures, LBOs, and financial killings.

Trevor Corcoran is the 40-year-old vice president of mergers and acquisitions for Teledynamics, a one-and-a-half-billion-dollar electronics and telecommunications conglomerate. By the time he reaches the office, his staff is waiting in the conference room for a 2:00 P.M. staff meeting he called at the last minute the day before.

Trevor opens the meeting, saying, "I confirmed at lunch today that Bergen Brunsway is selling its Thompson Electronics division. We want it. I have a package arriving tomorrow from Paine-Webber that analyzes the division's current situation. I'd like to start the due-diligence drill this afternoon. I have already talked with Shuman (Teledynamics' CEO). We have a green light if we can agree on terms. I'm having lunch with Bergen's president tomorrow. I'd like your preliminary analysis of terms by 11:00 A.M. Any questions?"

Research director Chanela Wilkes raises her hand. "How much over book value are we willing to pay?"

"As little as possible. Based on what we already know about Thompson, Bergen shouldn't be expecting much of a premium."

"What about the Chadwick deal?"

"Let's back off for now. A cool-down period might rekindle their motivation."

Trevor looks around the room. "Anything else? Okay, let's do it."

After the staff meeting, Trevor leaves the office for the country club to meet the other three members of his foursome for a round of golf—Brian Hughes, senior vice president at BankAmerica and relationship banker for Teledynamics; Eric Gunn, senior vice president at Goldman Sachs, the company's lead investment banker; and Peter Nulty, senior partner at O'Melvyny & Myers, the company's law firm. During the next four hours, Trevor chats casually with his companions, learning about the latest deal-making schemes and negotiating nuances. Trevor knows by experience and instinct that his relationship with these three people can make or break Teledynamics' merger and acquisition strategy, but he also immensely enjoys their company. He usually meets them once a week somewhere in the country for golf, sailing, a 49ers game, fishing, hunting, or a dinner date. Today, he finishes the round with a 93, third among the foursome. Last week, he caught the most rainbow trout during a fishing trip on the Snake River in Idaho.

At 7:00 P.M., Trevor and Eric Gunn meet their wives, Candice and Sally, for dinner at Josef's before a late symphony performance. Trevor's day finally comes to an end around 12:30 A.M., as he and Candice lie in bed discussing Chase's temper tantrum at the babysitter's.

Trevor Corcoran is a born NetWorker, filling every day with relationship-building activities that increase his competence. His ever-increasing network of friends and colleagues provides both personal satisfaction and a wealth of information because he follows a simple credo:

THE NETWORKER'S CREDO

I look constantly for opportunities to associate with talented people, building strong relationships with them in order to increase my own competence. I bring an honest respect to those with whom I associate, and I constantly strive to honor the needs and rights of all the people with whom I interact.

This attitude enables NetWorkers to construct webs of relationships that stimulate learning and growth. Taken to the extreme, however, this dimension of work can mislead one into thinking that as long as a person keeps talking to people and making friends, results will take care of themselves. Although you may wish to become skilled in this dimension of work, you should avoid the temptation to let it become an end in itself, depriving you of the benefits of the other dimensions, PowerWorking and ValueWorking. In this chapter, we look closely at how you can tap the full potential of this Second Dimension of work without letting it erode your ability to become a MetaWorker.

NETWORKING

On a Friday night in 1987, Hyrum Smith opened the door to his modest suburban home and greeted his wife with a weary smile. "I'm tired, really tired," he said, as he slumped into an overstuffed chair. He could see the look of concern on his wife's face. He'd come home exhausted before, especially since founding his own business three years earlier, but not without his usual abundance of energy. Smith tried to explain his exhaustion: "I taught three days of seminars to Kodak employees in Rochester; then I flew to New York for a dinner meeting with Merrill Lynch executives who had heard about our seminar; then I went on to Detroit for two more days of seminars with GM employees. Next week looks the same. Our program is catching on, but I can't keep up this pace. Success is fatiguing."

By the mid-1990s, Hyrum Smith had become the chairman and CEO of Franklin Quest, a $220 million international time management training company and the manufacturer of the Franklin Day Planner. However, back in 1987, Smith's struggling venture faced the same dilemma that plagues most start-up companies: How can the company duplicate the unique talents and skills of the original founder while adding new capabilities the organization needs to meet increasing and changing customer demand? For Hyrum Smith, that Friday night marked the beginning of an answer to that question.

As the company's star "performer," Hyrum Smith had raised the simple concept of time management to a new level by teaching a four-hour seminar that gave attendees a way to "gain control of their lives." His unique talent for spinning yarns mixed with humor and concepts captivated listeners with the idea of control and the goal of gaining "inner peace." After a four-hour seminar, most listeners would rush to thank the man who had opened their eyes to a better way of living and working. Many wrote letters expressing gratitude for his tutelage and promising to buy more Franklin Day Planner materials. As demand grew, the small company's management team wondered whether anyone besides the charismatic Smith could teach the seminar. In a very real sense, they knew that the company sold the unique talents of Hyrum Smith, as much as it sold his time management concepts.

"I simply knew that I possessed a unique talent to speak and train others," remembers Hyrum. "It was a talent that I had worked on and developed over many years. Looking back,

I wasn't sure whether anyone could easily duplicate that talent, but we simply had to have others teaching in order to grow the business."

As one of the first steps toward resolving the dilemma, Smith recruited Bob Lodie, a top sales manager for General Electric. Lodie recalls, "I think it was the challenge of trying to be as good as Hyrum that first attracted me." Preparing day and night, Lodie learned every nuance of the seminar, watched videotapes of Hyrum Smith in action, and perfected his pacing and "staging" of the program. Still, Lodie soon realized that he could not just parrot Smith; he had to internalize the seminar's teachings himself in order to come across as honest and genuine.

Prior to Lodie's first seminar, the client expressed disappointment that Hyrum Smith would not appear in person, but reluctantly agreed when the company assured him that Bob Lodie would do a great job. Nervously insecure, Lodie couldn't judge how well the seminar was going, even though his disciplined preparation and natural charm enabled him to move through the program smoothly. At the end of the day, however, as he scanned the evaluations from the attendees, he was thrilled to see that every one of the participants gave the seminar the highest possible rating, "10" on a scale of 10.

"It was on that day," recounts Hyrum, "after I heard about Bob's high evaluations, that I realized I could be duplicated. I also knew then that if we could find one Bob Lodie, we could find others."

In the years that followed, finding and developing presentation talent have become the hallmark of Franklin Quest. Having crafted detailed personality profiles of what makes good seminar presenters, the company annually reviews countless videotapes sent in by men and women who hope to become Franklin trainers. After initial screening, each applicant goes through a rigorous series of interviews with training managers, which culminate in a "trial performance." Those who pass the test receive extensive training in the Franklin way of teaching from the elite corps of Franklin trainers who deliver time management seminars around the world. "Hyrum's still the master," observed a recent new hire, "but now he uses his skills to teach us."

However, to secure Franklin's future back in the late 1980s, the company found that it needed to do more than just duplicate Hyrum Smith's talents; it needed to acquire and develop new talents as well. In the beginning, Franklin's training consultants did the selling, too. After completing a seminar, the trainer would contact the client and attempt to arrange follow-up seminars for the rest of the client's organization, making it unnecessary for Franklin Quest to field a separate sales and training force. Word of mouth and conscientious follow-up kept business flowing in.

Of course, no market remains static. As demand for Franklin's program increased, so did the competition. According to one client, "Within two years from the first training seminar with Franklin, I had other companies knocking on my door offering the same thing. Questions started coming down from my supervisors about why I was only using Franklin . . . why not any others? I suddenly had to justify my choice. I needed more information on why Franklin was better than the rest."

Unfortunately, Franklin's training consultants couldn't easily counter that objection, even though, out of sheer resourcefulness, they did assemble fact sheets and black and white sales brochures on their personal computers. According to Gary Leavitt, one of Franklin's early training consultants, "We had sales quotas given to us by upper management. They expected me to meet the sales quotas, plus teach all the seminars I sold. Keeping the pipeline full of prospects was virtually impossible. I found that during my seminars I would be thinking of who I had to call next. I would rush out to a phone during the breaks to close a sale. What worried me most was that I wasn't doing either job well. My seminar evaluations were lower and I wasn't closing many sales. It was a frustrating and difficult time. I seriously thought of leaving the company."

Competitors began making inroads into Franklin's market because the company's training consultants, busy teaching seminars, could not effectively handle inquiries from prospective clients. Finally, the company realized that its continued growth hinged on hiring marketing and sales people with the talent and drive to sell, make cold calls, follow up on prospects, and doggedly pursue new business. At the same time, the company resolved that it would not hamper the quality of training by burdening trainers with excessive demands. As Hyrum Smith recalls, "I remember sitting in our board room after a lengthy discussion and deciding that we couldn't ask our trainers to both sell and train. We needed to divide them into two groups. It seems like a 'no-brainer' now, but back then, it was a difficult decision. It affected how people were paid, altered career paths, and changed the type of people we attracted to the company."

As a first step, Franklin invited each training consultant to decide whether he or she wanted to teach or sell seminars. That put some people, such as Bob Lodie, in a difficult position. "I had a hard time with the decision," he recalls. "I thoroughly enjoyed training and it gave me a lot of satisfaction, but I realized that selling was my first love and my greatest personal strength. I chose to become a sales person. I've never looked back."

Eventually, the company divided its efforts to attract and develop talent for these two functions. As a result, the sales force has continued to expand aggressively while the field of training consultants has achieved new levels of excellence. The nurturing of both training and selling skills and their successful integration has created a company that recently ranked number 5 on the *Business Week* list of 100 Best Small Companies in America, number 12 on the *Forbes* list of Best Small Companies in the World, and number 2 on the *Equities Magazine* list of Fastest-Growing Companies on the New York Stock Exchange. Today, the company employs more than 2,000 people, ships products to over 150 countries, staffs offices in eight countries, trains more than 25,000 people attending 350 seminars in 200 cities each month, and serves several thousand corporate clients, including many *Fortune* 500 firms.

THE BASICS OF NETWORK

People can do amazing things all by themselves. Moya Chiburdanidze of the former Soviet Union won the women's world chess championship in 1978 at the age of 17; Ashrita Furman of Jamaica set a pogo stick jumping distance record of 13.06 miles (in 5 hours, 23 minutes) on September 15, 1989, in New York; also in New York, David Stein blew the world's biggest bubble—50 feet long—in 1988; and Lori Adams, 21, earned a place in *The Guiness Book of World Records* by tossing a rolling pin 175 feet during the 1979 Iowa State Fair. One enterprising young man, Roy Judd of Fort Worth, Texas, won a 1995 cherry-red GMC Sonoma pickup truck on September 25, 1994, by keeping his lips pressed against the side of the vehicle for 52 hours. Judd kissed his way to victory when two other contestants nodded off and lost lip position. "I didn't really need the truck," Judd told reporters. "I guess I did it to prove to myself I could keep up with the youngsters."

Other world-class achievements, however, require a team effort. True NetWorkers, modeling the Franklin Quest organization, can accomplish what no individual can. In an 18-year span between 1947 and 1964, the New York Yankees won an astonishing 15 American League Championships and 10 World Series; the UCLA Bruins captured 11 National Basketball Championships, 5 of them in a row, in the late 1960s and early 1970s. And who can forget the stirring underdog victory of the U.S. Men's Hockey Team when it beat the USSR for the Gold Medal at the 1980 Winter Olympics in Lake Placid?

No single person could build a nuclear submarine, either. On Sunday, September 25, 1994, First Lady Hilary Rodham Clinton christened the new nuclear attack submarine, Columbia, in Groton, Connecticut. Said Mrs. Clinton, "The teamwork it required to build a nuclear submarine involves the same kind of attitude my husband hopes to inspire in Americans. Every one of you knows your work cannot be sloppy, it can't be rushed, and it can't be done in a vacuum." Nicely spoken words, but, to the First Lady's chagrin, she then failed at PowerWork: It took her three swings to break a bottle of sparkling water against the sub's stern and send it sliding down the ramp on its maiden voyage.

Some PowerWorkers, such as former Los Angeles Lakers' center, Kareem Abdul Jabbar, also develop superb NetWorking, while some NetWorkers, such as the legendary coach of the

UCLA Bruins basketball team, John Wooden, also do first-rate PowerWork. Jabbar set records both in scoring and in assisting his teammates to score, and Wooden has won entrance into the Basketball Hall of Fame in Springfield, Massachusetts, as both a player and a coach.

Again, there are a few basics that make up NetWorking:

- The major goal of NetWork
- The common focus of NetWorkers
- The essential knowledge for NetWorking
- The strong bias in NetWork

Let's take a look at each.

---

1. THE MAJOR GOAL OF NETWORK

◆ NetWork focuses on the major goal of unifying the talents and abilities of the individual, the team, or the entire organization in a way that creates greater personal and collective *competence.*

◆ Two simple questions can help you focus your attention on NetWorking's major goal:

- What additional talents and capabilities do we need?
- How can we build relationships to better achieve common purpose and unity?

◆ You can usually recognize a NetWorking goal by its focus on developing people, building competence, or achieving common purpose.

◆ NetWorking goals help you promote and apply diverse capabilities that increase competence at all levels.

Karmin DeWald oversees the development of new product ideas and concepts at 3M Corporation, and he does it through effective NetWorking. Each year DeWald, with the express purpose of expanding 3M's product development competence, regularly recruits new scientists and technical experts graduating from the best schools. The minute new recruits arrive, they begin learning the 3M approach to doing things in a way that satisfies their own desire to contribute. The training encourages them to work in informal teams formed around new ideas and technologies, and it introduces them to the concept of bootlegging, whereby they "steal" away a portion of their time and company resources to work on projects of their choice. The entire system of the 3M Corporation promotes the talent development and relationship building that forms the company's competence. DeWald's major responsibility revolves around building individual and collective competence. He works privately and individually with the researchers, coaching and carefully channeling the efforts of each into those areas of discovery the company deems most potentially productive, while he looks constantly for new combinations of individuals to develop more applications of adhesives to flat plain surfaces. Although 3M's innovation focus may appear on the surface to cover a very narrow band, it actually places a premium on the talents and relationships of hundreds of people, allowing the company to routinely introduce hundreds of new products each year, thereby making itself competitively invincible through superior competence.

2. THE COMMON FOCUS OF NETWORKERS

◆ NetWorkers are skilled at *nurturing* the talent development of people and *integrating* the competencies of a group or organization for increased overall strength and capability. They relish forming relationships with others who seem more intelligent, more experienced, or more perceptive than themselves.

◆ You can become a better nurturer and integrator by continuously

• Seeking out underdeveloped or unapplied talents in yourself or others for further development and application.
• Striking the best possible alignment of talents, relationships, and challenges.
• Breaking down the barriers to the necessary talent development and relationship building that will increase individual, team, and organizational competence.

◆ You can recognize NetWorkers by the way they carefully catalog people's skills and capabilities, stay in close touch with a web of contacts, and constantly strive for optimum combinations of unique people.

◆ Effective nurturing and integrating expand people's capabilities and competence to meet the demands of a changing marketplace, stay ahead of the competition, and adjust to major industry or economic upheavals.

A number of new firms have been cashing in on the emergence of NetWorking as a vital dimension of work in today's team-oriented, nonhierarchical business environment. The Covey Leadership Center has done particularly well in this regard. With the best-selling book, *The Seven Habits of Highly Effective People,* over 200 weeks on *The New York Times* Best-Seller List, fueling the company's growth, The Covey Leadership Center has influenced millions of people around the world. With more than 500 employees and 7,500 licensed teachers and trainers facilitating video-based training, the company will top $100 million in revenues this year.

More than anything else, the Covey Leadership consulting and training program teaches individuals and organizations how to build talents and relationships through nurturing and integrating. A list of clients who love what Covey Leadership has done for their people reads like a Who's Who of Corporate America.

In one case, Saturn Corporation, the revolutionary division of General Motors, credits Covey for much of its success. Stephen Covey spoke to the company's scant 50 employees five years ago. His ideas about "sharpening the saw" (nurturing your talents) and "win-win thinking" (integrating complementary relationships) have helped shape Saturn's culture. According to Gary High, Saturn's manager of human resource development, more than 9,000 people have gone through Covey's training in recent years, giving the company a common language and approach to helping each other excel individually and succeed collectively. In terms of the relationship between management and the union, for years a source of frustration and resentment for automakers, at Saturn, management can't win if labor loses. Even assembly line workers believe the slogan: "At Saturn, we build people as well as cars."

Stephen Covey attributes his firm's phenomenal growth to "helping people build mutual trust on the basis of personal trustworthiness and then aligning structures and systems." Covey Leadership trains people around the world to become NetWorkers who know exactly how to nurture and integrate talents in any situation. Stephen Covey exemplifies the successful NetWorker.

3. THE ESSENTIAL KNOWLEDGE FOR NETWORKING

♦ NetWork demands knowing which talents (skills, capabilities, competencies) and relationships (mentoring, connections, direct reports, informal and formal teams, alliances, partnerships) will most successfully establish greater competence and common purpose.

> ◆ You can to stay knowledgeable about NetWork by constantly asking a single question: What else can we do to make sure that this combination of talents and relationships builds greater competence and achieves common purpose?
>
> ◆ You can trust that you are gaining knowledge for NetWorking when you become intimately familiar with your own, your team's, and your organization's talents and relationships and the way they intertwine.
>
> ◆ Effective NetWorking gives you the leverage to increase individual, team, and organizational competence through ever-expanding relationships.

In 1993, Dow Chemical Company created a new job: director of intellectual asset management. The idea for the job had grown out of an awareness over the years that although Dow's employees had successfully made new discoveries and filed 29,000 patents on those discoveries, the company had not actually implemented a large percentage of those patents, which had become "lost within the system." The primary competence of the company became neglected because NetWorking had been mismanaged. As reported in *Fortune* magazine, Gordon Petrash, the executive at Dow who became the new director of intellectual asset management, observed, "Patents aren't the only intellectual assets." Art and know-how (i.e., individual talents and working relationships), he believed, must also come into play.

Petrash found that Dow exploited fewer than half of its patents, many of which lacked an organizational home, someone who could care for them and maximize their market value. To rectify that situation, Petrash developed a six-step process for managing intellectual assets. The first step begins with strategic competence: Define an intellectual talent development strategy "for instance, the importance of intellectual investments to develop new products versus brick and mortar spending to achieve economies of scale." The second step assesses competitor strategies and knowledge assets, and the third classifies the company's talents and relationships: "What do we have? What do we use? Where does it belong?" The fourth step evaluates the company's assets: "What are the assets worth? What do they cost? What will it take to maximize their value? Should they be kept, sold, or abandoned?" The fifth step invests in filling any gaps by integrating company efforts to exploit past discoveries, shore up weak discoveries, and discover new knowledge that will keep the company moving ahead. The sixth step assembles the new knowledge portfolio and repeats the process.

"Just making intellectual asset management an explicit task pays benefits," reports *Fortune.* "When Dow discovered a new way to make polyolefin plastics used in coating wire and cables, the six-step process led the company to plan its research and write its patent in ways that make it tough for rivals to work around Dow."

4. THE STRONG BIAS IN NETWORK

♦ NetWorkers are always *developers* of people and organizations.

♦ To augment your NetWorking ability, we suggest the following:

- Spend time in introspection, assessing the development and application of your own talents and abilities.
- Get outside yourself and spend time with other people; learn from them and share your learning.
- Watch for opportunities to expand and deepen relationships that promise mutual growth.

♦ You can spot natural NetWorkers by the way they stress the "win-win relationship" as the key to progress.

♦ Building a stronger bias toward developing talents and relationships means getting more involved with other people.

Ralph Waldo Emerson, the father of Transcendentalism and a major figure in American Literature, reminds us in his essay "Self-Reliance," "There is a time in every man's [woman's] education when he [she] arrives at the conviction that envy is ignorance; that imitation is suicide; the he [she] must take himself [herself] for better, for worse, as his [her] portion; that though the wide universe is full of good, no kernel of nourishing corn can come to him [her] but through his [her] toil bestowed on that plot of ground which is given to him [her] to till. The power which resides in him [her] is new in nature, and none but he [she] knows what that is which he [she] can do, nor does he [she] know until he [she] has tried."

Conviction to nurture a talent and offer it up to respected colleagues for inclusion in a common purpose does not come easily for most people. If you naturally shy away from such an undertaking, keep trying, at the very least, to align yourself with natural NetWorkers. Their undying quest for self-discovery and self-deployment may well rub off on you, but even if it doesn't, your relationship with them will add immeasurable strength to your team or organization.

Not everyone exhibits superior talent for NetWorking, and not everyone possesses the intuition for NetWorking. If you consider yourself a natural NetWorker with underdeveloped capabilities, you can gain steady ground with a self-improvement program such as the one outlined later in this chapter. If you feel comfortable with this dimension of work, you can quite easily improve your talents and relationships.

However, if you do not consider yourself to be a natural NetWorker, you may want to spend more time with this chapter. Anyone can become a better NetWorker. By the same token, simply understanding the NetWork dimension can benefit PowerWorkers or ValueWorkers in team and organizational settings where they may find themselves relying more heavily on the contribution of natural NetWorkers.

In the final analysis, no individual, team, or organization can build competence without the constant and genuine development of talent and relationships. All of the people we have met in this chapter so far—Hyrum Smith, Karmin DeWald, Stephen

Covey, and Gordon Petrash—illustrate the benefits of developing NetWork. You can reap those benefits yourself by first evaluating then expanding your own talent and relationship developing abilities.

EVALUATING NETWORK

According to the legendary strategist, Sun Tzu, original author of *The Art of War,* skillful warriors first make themselves invincible and then wait for the enemy's moment of vulnerability. The key lesson in this ancient wisdom for NetWorking is that invincibility depends on yourself, your team, and your organization, whereas vulnerability depends on your competitors. Any NetWork improvement program must be preceded by a careful assessment of your ability to develop talents and relationships. You can conduct a detailed self-assessment of your NetWorking ability by answering the following questions for yourself, your team, and/or your organization (Fig. 3.1). A score between 45 and 60 represents outstanding NetWorking; scores between 30 and 44 reveal a need for continuous improvement; any scores between 15 and 29 indicate a need for major changes; and a score of 14 or below reflects a need for a substantial adjustment in your attitude toward your work.

The NetWorkers you encounter in this chapter would all score high on this test, probably close to 60. Regardless of the score you award yourself, your team, or your organization, you can take immediate steps to improve or maintain it.

EXPANDING NETWORK

Those of you who scored below 45 should take a minute to muse about the following fable. This is a story about four people with the names Everybody, Somebody, Anybody, and Nobody. There was an important job to be done, and Everybody was

Figure 3.1.   NetWork self-assessment.

For the period beginning _____, and ending _____,
answer the following questions by circling the number on the continuum that
best describes your assessment of NetWork during that period:

	Yes			Somewhat			No
1. Did you nurture your own talents?	6	5	4	3	2	1	0
2. Did you work to integrate your team's collection of talents?	6	5	4	3	2	1	0
3. Have you increased your organization's overall capabilities or competence?	6	5	4	3	2	1	0
4. Have your efforts increased your organization's competitive advantage?	6	5	4	3	2	1	0
5. Did you constantly evaluate whether the application of your talents was appropriate?	6	5	4	3	2	1	0
6. Did your team make progress toward better deploying the talents and skills of its members?	6	5	4	3	2	1	0
7. Did you improve your ability to build common purpose into your relationships?	6	5	4	3	2	1	0
8. Did you experience greater unity with your co-workers?	6	5	4	3	2	1	0
9. Have you spent quality time every-day NetWorking?	6	5	4	3	2	1	0
10. Do you consider yourself a better NetWorker now than you did at the beginning of this period?	6	5	4	3	2	1	0

sure that Somebody would do it. Anybody could have done it, but Nobody did it. Somebody got angry about that, because it was Everybody's job. Everybody thought Anybody could do it, but Nobody realized that Everybody wouldn't do it. As it ended up, Everybody blamed Somebody when Nobody did what Anybody could have done!

Even if you scored above 45 on the NetWork self-assessment, don't lull yourself onto easy street. Concentration and vigilance will be required to maintain a high level of talent and relationship development. Of course, if you scored below 45, you should embark on a program of improvement today by following three sequential steps: selecting, cultivating, and partnering.

Step 1. *Selecting: Identify the Capabilities You Need for Superior Performance.* The first step to improving Net-Work involves identifying the talents and skills needed to achieve distinctively superior results. In order to attract, build, develop, and coordinate capabilities, you must weigh changing needs in a constantly fluctuating external market and internal organizational environment. In other words you must ask, "What capabilities will lead to superior performance today, tomorrow and the day after tomorrow?" In your quest to monitor these capabilities, you should concentrate on the two categories of capabilities that most often create advantage:

- Those capabilities most essential to producing the right result
- Those capabilities most difficult for you to develop

In this process of selecting the necessary capabilities, remember that needs and circumstances change. For example, if a softball team will face more left-handed batters than usual this season, it will win more games if its pitching staff can strike out left-handed batters, and, if pitchers capable of shutting down left-handed batters are rare, the more switch hitters you develop, the greater batting advantage you will enjoy in your league. Anticipate future needs and changing circumstances, and you will improve your selections.

Step 2. *Cultivating: Diagnose Your Current and Desired Capabilities and How You Can Best Develop and Apply Them.* The second step begins with considering your unique capabilities and the work that lends itself best to those capabilities. You may determine that you possess more than one essential capability. In that case, you should ask yourself which one you can apply better than anyone else. You may also determine new capabilities that you can develop in order to perform new types of work.

To set the stage for relationship building, whether you choose to apply a current capability or develop a new talent, you should actively promote your capability to others who need the capability. In other words, let them know what you can do. It helps to think of yourself as a self-employed entrepreneur who must constantly market your capabilities, and constantly look for areas to apply what you do better than anyone else. You cannot develop true NetWork unless you recognize and contribute a unique and essential capability to a relationship that can produce a desired work outcome.

For example, if a ballet company lacks a principal dancer to portray the kind of emotion required in "Oephilia," and you have long cultivated the expression of passions in your dancing, then you must communicate to that ballet company your ability to infuse their troupe with precisely what they need. Together, both of you can flourish.

Keep in mind that few, if any, aspects of a person's work life remain static. Because work outcomes, methods, technologies, and skills change as often as the weather, a capability that makes a unique contribution today may lose its momentum tomorrow. Unrelenting change provides a constant wellspring of opportunity, and success requires an unending effort to recognize and build the abilities to make ever-new and unique contributions.

Step 3. Partnering: Complement Your Talents with Those of Others. The final step in developing NetWork involves shaping alliances. These alliances take two forms.

The first form requires that you align yourself with others who possess the capabilities you need today. In today's world of work, neither you nor your team nor your organization can control all the most advantageous capabilities essential for superior performance. The increasingly diverse specialization of knowledge and quickening pace of change make it uneconomical, if not impossible, for anyone to try to be an expert in everything. The trend toward outsourcing in the corporate world proves that business leaders will go wherever necessary to acquire the capabilities they need. It makes less and less economic sense to invest in developing an internal capacity that you presently need but lack, especially if that need will soon change.

The second form of alliance entails aligning yourself with those who possess talent that you may need tomorrow. The resulting combination can generate even greater capability and advantage in the future. The capabilities of such alliances accrue geometrically, not arithmetically, because resulting competence creates a synergy that forms new combinations and new areas of performance not currently envisioned. More than becoming "self-directed" or "self-empowered," Net-Working means working in a "jobless society" where everyone is "self-employed," all marketing their talents with each other. Only by unleashing our true capabilities, continually developing them, and aligning ourselves in a myriad of partnerships can we succeed in the new world of work.

These three steps of selecting, cultivating, and partnering become even more important in the new world of the Internet, where decision making will continue its transfer from the executive suite to the frontliner's desktop. Empowered teams of people involved in strategic and operational projects will make more and more of the critical decisions on which success depends. Moreover, while traditional meetings will never completely disappear, technology will greatly alter the meetings of the future.

Companies such as IBM, Wang, Digital, Microsoft, Novell, and NetScape are already creating NetWorking systems that will facilitate wiser decisions through groupware and meetingware. Products, such as CM/I from Corporate Memory Systems, employ a combination of meeting facilitation and technology to create a map of the decision-making process that captures the thought processes involved in every important decision. Another product, CA Facilitator from Mccall, Szerdy & Associates, tracks the rapid flow of ideas that result from brainstorming sessions. Team Talk from Trax Softworks makes it possible for an organization to develop knowledge bases and discussion databases on a wide variety of topics. Such products will make the three steps of NetWorking even more vital in the future. With them, selecting talents and skills, cultivating talents and skills through strategically crafted relationships, and constantly partnering through relationships that can bring superior performance, now and in the future, will become easier and easier.

Already, Allianz Life, a German-owned, Minneapolis-based life insurance company, uses IBM's Time and Place/2 Group Calendaring and Scheduling software to coordinate the activities of 750 employees in five different locations. By technologically calendaring and scheduling meetings, planning sessions, and performance evaluations, Allianz's new system is a technological alternative to personal planners, minimizing coordination hassles and pushing project management to new heights. In such environments, successful NetWorking becomes every worker's key to forging common purpose, finding fulfillment, and getting results.

When his associates describe Dr. Michael Paul, they invariably mention his continual drive to stretch himself, push his personal knowledge, try new ideas, experiment with new technologies, and welcome change.

Dr. Paul works as a freelance project manager, overseeing the development of interactive CD-ROM learning programs. He has formed working relationships with a close circle of multimedia production houses where he manages teams of creative professionals engaged in the production of titles ranging from interactive instruction in surgical procedures to point-of-sale kiosks for firearms companies. With a causal, yet deeply involved style, he directs teams along a desired path, sensitively stroking the tender egos of software programmers, meeting the mad rush of production deadlines, and guaranteeing the creative freedom needed by education curriculum designers. He participates in management meetings, bridging the "black box" gap that exists between the business side and the creative side in this fledgling industry, carefully instructing management in understandable terms about the technical complexities that surround each CD-ROM product.

"I started out as a dentist," Paul confesses, "All of my education was in the sciences—chemistry, botany and the like. I graduated from Loyola Dental School and had a successful dental practice for many years."

As Dr. Paul talks about his new field of work, it becomes clear that his overarching talent for instructing and educating others has always threaded through his endeavors. "I found that I could relax from working all day in people's mouths by teaching night classes at the local college. I taught the basics of dentistry to dental hygienists and loved it. And I was good at it." In fact, Dr. Paul received commendations from students and faculty alike for his ability to explain highly technical material in terms they could easily grasp. His clear perception of what people needed to know and a burning desire to communicate that knowledge fueled his drive for innovation. "I could see the subject so clearly, and knew exactly what needed to be communicated, but words alone were not enough to get the students to see it the way I did. I knew there was a better way."

Frustrated with both the constraints of his dental practice and the limitations of academic lectures, he closed his dental practice and entered a doctoral program in Educational Design. For the next two years, Dr. Paul became engrossed in the nuances of how people learn and the mediums that enhance their learning.

He recalls his first attempt at automated instruction: "I was still teaching on the side and got a grant to experiment with video-assisted training. This was a few years before any of the real advances in computer technology. I hooked up a computer to a videotape machine, sequenced some video segments of a surgery, and built a tutorial for a student." No one had ever designed a system quite like it. Students read text from a computer screen on which video sequences related to the text appeared periodically. When a student answered a set of questions at the end, the proper video segment reappeared to reinforce learning. The students loved the self-paced, less-confrontive approach.

Paul now says, "Looking back, the system was very slow and cumbersome. It was definitely limited. But it showed me the great potential for the future." Over the next few years, he continued to experiment and refine the system. "Because of my interest, I soon found that business people were coming to the college to find out about me and talk with me. Many had far more resources than the college, and some of them were very interested in getting into this type of training commercially."

Paul soon left the university and aligned himself with one of the inquiring companies, where he refined his skills and enhanced his knowledge of technology, concentrating much of his time on data compression and educational design. Although he soon discovered that he would never become a world-class programmer himself, his teaching background and intimate knowledge of technology allowed him to NetWork with top programmers, whose skills he needed and who, in turn, respected his skills.

Looking back on his success, he concludes, "I have always kept up to speed with the advances of technology, CD-ROM technology, data compression, video capture, and authoring technologies for multimedia. This has been a passion for me as well as a requirement. If I had ever stopped developing my skills, I wouldn't be working today. I am sure that I will always have to be in a mode of developing my capabilities. That seems to be a requirement in my business. And as I look back, I never would have guessed that my career would have taken me through so many fields. But each move has opened a new door of opportunity. I enjoyed walking through them all."

As a consummate NetWorker, Dr. Michael Paul has built a satisfying and multifaceted career out of his passion for developing talents and relationships.

✔ NetWorkers are developers, lifelong learners, and re-lationship builders.

✔ Networkers use the skills of nurturing and integrating to select needed capabilities, cultivate talents and rela-tionships, and partner with whoever can add more competence.

✔ Consistently developing talents and relationships leads to greater individual and collective competence.

✔ NetWork promotes building greater competence as the best way to increase competitive advantage and economic success in the intermediate and long term.

✔ Even if you are not a natural NetWorker, you can improve your NetWorking by implementing Net-Working's three stages: selecting, cultivating, and part-nering. Remember, *you* are responsible for developing the competence necessary for your success.

CHAPTER FOUR

ValueWorkers

"Creativity can solve almost any problem. The creative act, the defeat of habit by originality, overcomes everything."

George Lois

A DAY IN THE LIFE OF A VALUEWORKER

"Aha!" Asleep one minute, completely awake the next, Hadley Mead (a fictional character) leaps out of bed at 3:00 A.M., and fumbles for his glasses on the dresser.

Startled, his wife, Anne, murmurs, "Having a brainstorm again?" Her tone of voice suggests that this happens all the time.

"Uh-huh," mutters her husband. "Be right back."

As Hadley belts his bathrobe and dashes out of the room, Anne smiles and falls contentedly back to sleep.

Flipping on the light in his study, Hadley pulls out a yellow legal pad to capture his dream before it escapes. For the past week, he has been concentrating on achieving a breakthrough for the next version of IdeaScape, one of his company's presentation software products, and tonight he thinks he finally may have discovered it.

Hadley Mead is a Pacific Northwesterner to the core. Born and raised in Seattle, he cofounded MeadMyer Software shortly after graduating with a degree in electrical engineering from the University of Washington. For an hour he scribbles notes and diagrams on his legal pad, outlining his idea for using learning theory and psychological preferences to adapt the next version of IdeaScape to a variety of different audiences, situations, cultures, and objectives. Finally, he enters it all into his Macintosh.

Returning to bed at 5:30 A.M., Hadley sleeps until 9:00 A.M., when he awakes for the second time, pondering his nocturnal illumination. It still looks good. From 9:00 A.M. to 12:00 noon, he sits at his computer, toying with a number of alternative designs for his new "audience-adaptation" feature. At noon, he calls the office to say he won't be in today. His assistant, Moira Bowen, reminds him of his 3:00 P.M. meeting with his partner, Paul Myer; the company's new controller, Devin Dursteller; and a group of outside auditors.

Hadley groans. "I forgot. Paul can handle it."

"He has already rescheduled the meeting twice so you can be there."

"Tell him I've found the key to IdeaScape 3.0. That'll make him happy."

A giggle tickles Hadley's ear. "You're hopeless," says Moira.

"Tell the accountants I've found a way to double our revenues next year, but not if I waste time in this meeting."

"I'll take care of it."

"Thanks. And, uh . . . maybe you should cancel my appointments for the rest of the week."

After hanging up the phone, Hadley suggests lunch to Anne, who eagerly accepts. At their favorite nearby restaurant, Hadley shares his breakthrough with Anne, and by the time their entrés arrive, the conversation turns to what Anne will be teaching her ancient world history class that afternoon at Evergreen College. Over dessert, their conversation shifts to their three teenage children, all mired in the usual adolescent struggles.

During the afternoon, Hadley perfects his breakthrough, then calls Moira at the office just before 5:00 P.M. to ask her to set up a meeting in the morning with programmers Cheryl Riggs and Dil Chopak.

"Tell them to put everything else on hold," he says. "We've got work to do."

That evening, about 7:00 P.M., while Hadley and Anne watch their 16-year-old daughter play softball, he begins thinking about another pesky problem, upgrading DataSpread, the company's bestselling spreadsheet software. The distant look on his face tells Anne that his brain has once again left his body.

Hadley Mead epitomizes the natural ValueWorker, who devotes the lion's share of any given day to discovering new ideas. He knows that nothing will benefit his company more than the valuable contributions he keeps generating. A simple credo guides his work:

THE VALUEWORKER'S CREDO

I concentrate on new ideas, discoveries, and breakthroughs that will deliver more value to more people. I take risks in my work, always aiming to push beyond the status quo to a whole new level of understanding and accomplishment.

This emphasis on discovery enables the ValueWorker to pioneer new territory, but when it becomes an obsession, it can isolate a person from others, thus separating the ValueWorker from the resources that can turn a breakthrough idea into something that delivers tangible benefits to the world. If you desire to enter into this dimension of work, you must take care that it does not so preoccupy you that you abandon the other dimensions—PowerWorking and NetWorking. In this chapter, we scrutinize this third dimension of work in hope that you can master it for maximum benefit.

VALUEWORKING

In the homebuilding industry, thousands of independent local contractors construct half a dozen homes a year, hanging on during economic downturns and scrambling day and night when the economy gets hot. Although they provide the backbone of the industry, they have also developed a notoriety for exceeding budgets and missing deadlines, seemingly unconcerned about the inconvenience and frustration that cost overruns and delays cause their customers. Most homebuyers may accept this situation as "just the way it is," but one company, Centex Corporation, has been diligently ValueWorking to change all of that.

Headquartered in Dallas, Texas, Centex has quietly, yet quickly, become America's largest homebuilder, with revenues of more than three billion dollars and a mortgage lending division that ranks in the nation as a leading originator of single-family home mortgages. With more than 6,000 employees located in more than 200 offices in 23 states, Centex has turned the homebuilding industry on its head and povided a stimulating model for the future. Since 1969, when the company became publicly held, it has never reported a quarterly or annual loss or posted a major write-off. In the most simple terms, Centex believes in its own version of a familiar phrase: "Build a better house and the world will beat a path to your door." The company has been creating more value for more and more Americans each year for two decades by eliminating budget overruns and missed deadlines. In 1993 alone, Centex built more than 10,000 homes for Americans and began expanding its market into Mexico and abroad.

Since the mid-1980s, when CEO Larry Hirsch, COO Bill Gillilan, and CFO David Quinn joined forces to turn Centex's conglomeration of acquisitions into an integrated corporate culture and superior performer, Centex has fueled a trend toward corporate homebuilding throughout the United States. According to these three ValueWorking executives (a lawyer, a Harvard MBA, and a Big 6 accounting firm partner, respectively), "Building Strength," this year's theme, has multiple meanings at Centex. "*Building* Strength relates to the quality and integrity of the structures and products we create and the services we provide," says a Centex spokesperson. "Building *Strength* implies a consistent, ongoing focus on the development of our most valuable asset—the Centex people. Finally, *Building Strength* suggests our conservative financial management, which provides Centex with the resources to pursue its strategic objectives." Such solid commitment to building a corporate culture that provides greater homebuilding value to a greater number of homebuyers has produced impressive financial results with record revenues and earnings in 1993 and 1994.

Well aware of the effort it takes to maintain a strong culture in a decentralized company, Larry Hirsch and his colleagues follow a simple rule: "Since homebuilding is essentially a local business, controlling a geographically diverse builder of such size requires many creative, entrepreneurial people experienced in Centex's systematic approach to this complex business. Developing such people is at the core of our strategy."

A firsthand view of the Centex culture at an annual meeting of the company's top 75 executives and then at a subsequent conference with the top 60 executives in the homebuilding division, gave vivid proof of the company's precise and persistent emphasis on the dual demands of creativity and financial soundness, profit and growth, discipline and flexibility, systems and entrepreneurship, hammer and heart. The meetings, focused on the year 2000, stressed the importance of both management and leadership in order to continue creating more value for more customers. Endlessly discussing ways to make homebuilding and financing more affordable, enjoyable, accessible, profitable, and adaptable, the Centex executives obviously loved what they were doing and genuinely believed that they would develop ways to do it better in the future. They had enshrined ValueWorking as a central element of their work at Centex.

THE BASICS OF VALUEWORK

ValueWorkers discover breakthroughs that benefit people. The greatest breakthroughs benefit the greatest number. Working in every field of human endeavor, as inventors, marketers, architects, writers, filmmakers, builders, poets, artists, doctors, lawyers, teachers, thinkers, and leaders. ValueWorkers change the world by devising a better way, penning a classic work of literature, constructing an enduring edifice, fashioning a breaktaking sculpture, discovering a cure for a lethal disease, dreaming up a new philosophy, or leading a group or nation to breathtaking achievement. Their ranks include common people who make uncommon contributions: Thomas Edison, Henry Ford, Frank Lloyd Wright, Robert Frost, Ralph Waldo Emerson, Orson Wells, Frederich Olmstead, Pablo Picasso, Jonas Salk, John Dewey, and Franklin Delano Roosevelt. Yet thousands of less-heralded ValueWorkers add value to a great many lives every day. Who invented the paper clip? Who oversaw the construction of the interstate highway system? Who has brought American history alive for most high school students in this country? Few parents recognize the name Lewis Paul Todd, yet Todd wrote a history textbook, *The Rise of the American Nation,* first published in 1952, and now in its 11th edition, which has been read by more than 40,000,000 high school students.

ValueWorkers collect unconnected pieces of information in a way similar to a child storing fireflies in a bottle until the bottle is full and emits a brighter light. Then with that brighter light, the child finds a new path that leads off through the forest and bushes to a new place never seen before. ValueWorkers are not necessarily geniuses; they do not always become rich and famous; their contributions may go unrecognized and unrewarded, but they do reflect certain basics:

- The ultimate purpose of ValueWork
- The common concerns of ValueWorkers

- The prerequisite knowledge for ValueWorking
- The all-consuming bias in ValueWork

1. THE ULTIMATE PURPOSE OF VALUEWORK

◆ The ultimate purpose of ValueWork is *breakthrough,* a dramatic advance in knowledge or understanding that results in major product, performance, or progress improvements.

◆ Answering "yes" to the following three questions will improve your ValueWorking:

- Will you constantly question everything?
- Will you continually search for better ways?
- Will you always seek new insights and deeper understanding?

◆ You can always recognize those in pursuit of the ValueWorking purpose because they choose the path of discovery where stepping-stones often prove elusive. ValueWorkers never stop searching for new and better ideas or methods that challenge the status quo.

◆ ValueWorking not only comes from people who devote a large portion of their day to "thinking" or "research and development," but from ordinary people who seek a better way in their daily work.

True ValueWorkers understand that unapplied discoveries never create real value. Clover Club Foods, a $50 million regional snack food manufacturer, realized this during a series of strategy sessions in the early 1980s. Clover Club had defined its position in the market as number two behind Frito-Lay and had consequently related every strategic and tactical decision to its competitor. If Frito-Lay introduced a new garlic and onion potato chip, Clover Club would develop its own garlic and onion potato chip. If Frito-Lay added new trucks on a delivery route to improve customer service, Clover Club would do the same. Although Bob Sanders, Clover Club's CEO, took great pride in the company's number two position in the marketplace, he also wished to prepare the company for sale. He knew that he had to move the company to new levels of strategic planning and management.

Through a series of strategy sessions in which the company's senior management team of seven executives reviewed and considered applying the hottest new strategy concepts, Sanders zeroed in on Clover Club's positioning vis-à-vis Frito-Lay by asking pointed questions about the differences between Clover Club and its top competitor. Initially, he simply wanted to clarify and define Clover Club's position, but as the discussion unfolded, he saw the glimmering of a breakthrough: Clover Club could, in fact, move much faster in its market by experimenting with new products and markets. Whereas Frito-Lay needed a $50 million market to support a new product, Clover Club could profitably serve a $1- or $2-million market. Frito-Lay shunned lower- and higher-priced products, leaving unserved markets vulnerable for attack. However, because Clover Club had defined itself as number two behind Frito-Lay, it traditionally tried to copy whatever Frito-Lay did, without trying to differentiate itself from its top competitor. During one lively session, the insight struck like lightning: Clover Club should position itself as number one regionally instead of number two behind Frito-Lay nationally. When Sanders first broached the idea to the Clover Club executives, they seemed surprised, but as he explained its significance, they began to share his excitement.

Defining Clover Club's position as number one regionally would allow the company to duplicate some of Frito-Lay's strengths while exploiting its weakness. Clover Club could offer more product varieties faster and cheaper than Frito-Lay, and it could switch directions in a fraction of the time it took Frito-

Lay to do so. As Sanders discussed the notion, ideas sprang from the group: a new line of discounted tortilla chips, a revitalization of pork rinds, experimentation with sauces and dips, and a host of new seasonings and flavorings for both potato and tortilla chips.

Over the next several months, Clover Club developed a new strategy that took advantage of its number one position among regional competitors (better market penetration, brand awareness, customer loyalty) while exploiting Frito-Lay's weaknesses (market size parameters, slowness to market, narrow price parameters). The breakthrough gave Clover Club a whole new way of thinking about its strategic position and opportunities, and, within a year, Clover Club's new line of discounted and high-variety tortilla chips became the company's hottest seller. Frito-lay eventually responded with new varieties of tortilla chips, but it never succeeded in displacing Clover Club's new first position in its regional markets. Within two years, Bob Sanders capitalized on this achievement when he negotiated the lucrative sale of his company to Borden.

THE COMMON CONCERNS OF VALUEWORKERS

- ◆ ValueWorkers are successful *searchers* and *creators* who usually listen more than they talk, constantly ask questions of themselves and others, and never give up until their searching leads to the creation of a new breakthrough.

- ◆ To improve your searching and creating skills, you should

  - Never feel shy about revealing your own ignorance.
  - Devote a portion of each day to solitary time during which you can contemplate what new knowledge or understanding you have gained.

- Resist the temptation to "look busy" or "stay active" by taking confidence in the time you set aside for reading, thinking, or productive daydreaming.

♦ You can recognize ValueWorkers by their patience in searching and their commitment to creating. They know that true discovery and breakthroughs always take time and perseverance.

♦ Effective searching and creating transforms abstract ideas and thoughts into concrete breakthroughs—new products, services, approaches, processes, models, inventions, cures, and paradigms.

Trip Hawkins, CEO of the struggling 3DO Company, has always asked these sorts of questions, and when he started 3DO, he didn't just start a company—he created an industry. Driven by a vision to build a new, massive market based on multimedia games and entertainment wherein users could interact with life-like characters, Hawkins has been pursuing a course that will potentially influence the daily learning and leisure habits of hundreds of millions of people around the world. After building Electronic Arts, a successful $300 million company in San Mateo, with video games such as John Madden Football, Hawkins shifted his focus to a new company, 3DO, which creates ideas, then licenses them to more than 500 hardware and software companies. To get hardware manufacturers such as Panasonic, MCA, and Crystal Dynamics to build 3DO machines (i.e., multimedia players), Hawkins gives them the designs free of charge and provides technological help. Software companies that develop games and entertainment will pay 3DO a three-dollar royalty for each product sold. However, Hawkins knows that he must install multimedia players in half of the homes in America before 3DO will make any money.

Although Panasonic's first multimedia player, built with 3DO's help, has gotten off to a slow start, Hawkins refuses to relinquish his vision of creating more value for more people than any of his competitors. Many industry analysts think he'll eventually win, and win big, but there are no such guarantees when you're attempting to create a breakthrough. He recently summarized his philosophy to the business press this way: "The most brilliant ideas are not going to be understood by most people, are they? If you wait around to make decisions by democracy, you end up with a boring company, and eventually, it's going to kill you." Trip Hawkins knows what creating the greatest value for the greatest number means, so it's no surprise that he performs ValueWork every day of his life.

Wall Street analysts were once red hot on Hawkins and 3DO, but all that's changed. The company's stock now trades at $11, down from a high of $48 in October 1993. Regardless of how 3DO's products and future eventually fare, Trip Hawkins will keep searching for breakthroughs and creating value for customers. If 3DO dies, we fully expect to see a reincarnation of Trip Hawkins in some other CD-ROM venture striving for yet another breakthrough.

THE PREREQUISITE KNOWLEDGE FOR VALUEWORKING

♦ ValueWork requires understanding of both the worth and impact of a potential or actual breakthrough.

♦ You can ask three questions to increase your Value-Working knowledge:

- What are your customers' biggest problems, unmet needs, or desires for greater benefits?
- What are your company's greatest obstacles, unresolved issues, or challenges to progress?
- What are your competitors' most significant strengths and weaknesses, best practices, or missed opportunities?

> ◆ You can be assured you are developing the prerequisite knowledge for ValueWorking when you pay close attention to predicting or evaluating the ultimate worth and impact of your breakthrough.
>
> ◆ Effective ValueWorking allows you to carefully weigh the real value of a breakthrough and remain highly sensitive to exactly how customers, employees, competitors, suppliers, other stakeholders, and the general public will be affected.

In 1990, Soltech Audio (a disguised name), lured by the attractiveness of the audio sound system markets in the United States, relocated its company headquarters from Australia to America. Founder Dr. John Solavey (a pseudonym), an audio engineer who specialized in high-frequency radio transmissions used by various governments for secure radio communications, had won a large number of sophisticated and technical patents, which he proudly displayed on his office wall.

Although Solavey, now in his late 60s, loved his work, he had not yet reaped substantial rewards from it. When the fickle nature of working under government contracts forced Solavey to search for a more stable source of income, he decided to enter the stereo speaker business. "The first speaker that I marketed was actually a monitor that I had built as part of a communications system for one of my clients," Solavey recalls. "It received great reviews by the music critics as having an extremely high quality of sound and quickly established Soltech Audio. I branched out from there."

Reluctantly at first, but somewhat more aggressively over time, Solavey applied his unique technical talents to discovering new technologies for speaker systems and ended up producing a small, but highly regarded line of stereo speakers, which appealed to high-end audiophiles who could afford a product priced between $2,000 and $12,000 per pair.

After six months, however, Soltech's penetration into the U.S. market had stalled. As Scott Brenner, U.S. marketing manager for Soltech, remembers, "It was apparent that what the market wanted was changing." The demand for high-quality sound was expanding into the video business. "We were approached one day by the technicians at Lucas Films," explains Brenner. "They had a new concept of home entertainment called 'THX Home Theater.' This marked the very beginning of a marriage between high-quality video movies and high-end sound systems, and it had great market potential."

For years, George Lucas had pioneered a highly sophisticated split sound track for such films as "Star Wars" and "Indiana Jones" that resulted in a virtual reality experience for moviegoers. Background sounds emanated from speakers in the rear of the theater; powerful bass sounds poured out of two front speakers, and the actors' voices came from speakers located directly in front of the screen. The technique filled the theater with realistic sound that enhanced the intensity of the viewing experience.

Before long, moviegoers expected this same quality of sound when they watched the video at home, but they felt disappointed when the small speakers on their TVs didn't deliver. Research showed that people would pay for a higher-quality sound system.

Through the THX Home Theater technology, Lucas began working to bring this same high-quality sound into the home by combining elements of exclusive theater technology that decoded the soundtrack and sent it through a series of amplifiers and a set of five speakers. Although the approach promised increased entertainment value to the customer, it would not deliver that benefit without the right sort of speakers. That's when Soltech entered the picture.

According to Jim Kropolus, a technical specialist working for Lucas, "We knew that Dr. Solavey had the knowledge and expertise that was needed to discover the right application for home speakers. What we didn't know was whether Solavey would be willing to work with us on the project."

In fact, Solavey did not warm to the project at first. He presented a number of technical arguments showing why the concept would not work, saying, "No one will buy this system. Customers still want the traditional two-speaker, high-quality sound system." Although he wanted to continue developing new stereo models that appealed to only a small market, pressure from his U.S. partners to build revenue fast forced him to embark on the THX sound project, albeit halfheartedly.

"Throughout the entire effort Solavey was extremely difficult to work with," recalls Jim Kropolus. "He missed deadlines, argued about technical issues, and continued to claim this was all a waste of time because there was no market for it. We were getting frustrated with him."

Solavey's first test of a trial speaker system sounded fabulous. In a room the size of a typical family room in an average house, the system's surrounding sound filled the room. As airplanes flew on a large TV screen, the sound shot from the back speakers to the front as if the planes were actually passing directly overhead. The reverberation of gunshots echoed from the deep bass. The actors' dialog came through crisp and clear.

"I was impressed with the potential," remembers Kropolus, "but technically we still had some bugs to work out. There was one pesky technical problem in the audio range of the two front speakers that Solavey had not solved. The speakers he had designed just didn't extent far enough. We were missing critical sounds we felt we needed."

When confronted with the concern, Solavey gave up the search. Recalls Brenner, "I could see that Solavey was stumped. He couldn't redesign the speaker to meet the specifications. His pride kept him from asking the Lucas techniques for advice. In fact, he wouldn't accept any advice from anyone. That was probably his biggest mistake."

"Looking back," reflects Scott Brenner, "I think Solavey simply didn't buy into the fact that anyone wanted the technology. He didn't make the effort to work out the technical bugs. Technically it was a real challenge, and although he was searching for the solution, he couldn't bring it together. He began to argue that if he couldn't do it, no one could."

Before his frustrations with Solavey, George Lucas had initiated a similar project with another company. Through collaboration and a continual search for solutions, the other research team managed to break through the technology problem and design a speaker that could meet the specifications. The label of the other company appeared on the first THX Home Theater speaker system introduced into the marketplace.

Observes Brenner, "To this day, Solavey acts as if he doesn't care we missed the window. He complains that the market is too small and denies the fact that Home Theater has created great market reaction, perhaps the biggest hit in our business since stereo sound. We were on the leading edge of an incredible opportunity, but because of our inability to focus on what the customers really valued, we lost out." Within two years, Soltech closed its U.S. operations and sold all of its assets. Unfortunately for Soltech, Dr. Solavey failed in his evaluation of worth and impact.

4. THE ALL-CONSUMING BIAS IN VALUEWORK

♦ In the fullest sense, ValueWorkers are *discoverers*.

♦ To increase your ability to perform ValueWork, you should

- Display a fearlessness to proceed into new arenas.
- Be willing to take risks.
- Consider new options.
- Pursue uncharted paths.
- Relish the adventure of discovery.
- Probe every possibility.
- Become more fluid in your adaptability to change.
- Never be afraid to leave the past behind.

♦ You can identify natural ValueWorkers by the way they refuse to live within the limited securities of fixed systems and organizational purposes. They must always push the envelope past the boundaries and into the unknown.

♦ Becoming more consumed with "discovering" breakthroughs requires more time spent questioning the status quo.

Albert Einstein, unarguably one of the world's greatest discoverers, reminds us: "The development of science and of the creative activities of the spirit in general requires still another kind of freedom, which may be characterized as inward freedom. It is this freedom of the spirit which consists in the independence of thought from the restrictions of authoritarian and social prejudice as well as from unphilosophical routinizing and habit in general. This inward freedom is an infrequent gift of nature and a worthy objective for the individual. Yet the community can do much to further this achievement, too, at least by not interfering with its development."

Although discovering and creating new value does not come easily, even for the gifted, individuals, teams, and organizations can experience significant breakthroughs by acknowledging the importance of ValueWork and encouraging workers to spend time in that dimension. If you naturally retreat from such undertakings, keep trying, and, at the very least, align yourself with natural ValueWorkers. Their undying quest for knowledge and discovery may help you grow. If not, they will still add immeasurable strength to your team or organization.

Some people are natural ValueWorkers, possessing an innate ability to search for and create value. Born discoverers, they love the third dimension of work. It makes sense to them. Addicted to acquiring knowledge and hooked on storing up wisdom, natural ValueWorkers focus first and foremost on discovering breakthroughs that give them more control over their destiny. Whether scientists, engineers, teachers, philosophers, poets, logicians, or executives, natural ValueWorkers thirst for knowledge and understanding. Their "discovery of the universe" orientation serves them well when it comes to searching for knowledge, creating worth and value, and breaking through the status quo. Close associates often describe them as aloof, preoccupied, remote, and enigmatic. Those who are not natural ValueWorkers often fail to comprehend the deep need of natural ValueWorkers to comprehend reality and thereby break through to new levels of achievement. More appreciation of this fact will help both the natural ValueWorkers and those for whom ValueWork is not second nature.

Obviously, many of us are not born with the instinctive or pure talent for ValueWorking. If you consider yourself a natural ValueWorker with underdeveloped capabilities, you can gain steady ground with a self-improvement program such as the one outlined later in this chapter. Since you are comfortable with this dimension of work, you should be able to improve your searching and creating capabilities.

Simply understanding the ValueWork dimension can benefit you in team and organizational settings where you may find yourself relying more heavily on the contribution of natural ValueWorkers.

ValueWork focuses not only on discovering something of value, but also on affecting a large number of others with that value. It's like dropping a pebble in a pond. The larger the pebble (the value), the more ripples it sends to the shore. The larger the ripples, the more effect they produce for all those who surround the pond. Producing such ripple effects of value can pay big dividends in the form of profits, market share, reputation, and opportunity to whoever drops the pebble.

EXAMINING VALUEWORK

ValueWork can be pictured as meandering through the intricate and complicated technical network of the Internet, exploring one node of information, double clicking on another, entering a line in a forum discussion, E-mailing a new contact, and constantly pursuing a thread of light that will hopefully lead to some ultimately useful discovery.

Learning to assess such discovery skills can help you discover more ValueWork. Conduct a ValueWork self-examination (Figure 4.1) by answering the following questions. Scores between 45 and 60 indicate outstanding ValueWorking; scores between 30 and 44 reveal a need for continuous improvement; any score between 15 and 29 marks a need for major changes; and a score of 14 or below suggests the need for a substantial adjustment in the way you think about and perform your work.

Figure 4.1. ValueWork self-examination.

For the period beginning _____, and ending _____, answer the following questions by circling the number on the continuum that best describes your assessment of ValueWork during the period specified:

	Yes	Somewhat	No

1. Did you increase the value or benefits you deliver to customers or other stakeholders?

   Yes Somewhat No
   6 5 4 3 2 1 0

2. Did you increase the number of customers, employees, partners, or other recipients to whom you deliver value?

   Yes Somewhat No
   6 5 4 3 2 1 0

3. Have you consistently searched for breakthroughs?

   Yes Somewhat No
   6 5 4 3 2 1 0

4. Have you concentrated on creating value?

   Yes Somewhat No
   6 5 4 3 2 1 0

5. Did you focus on better understanding the worth of your products, services, or efforts?

   Yes Somewhat No
   6 5 4 3 2 1 0

6. Have you thoroughly considered the future needs, wants, and desires of those to whom you deliver value?

   Yes Somewhat No
   6 5 4 3 2 1 0

7. Did you improve your ability to discover knowledge, and apply it to create more value for more numbers of people?

   Yes Somewhat No
   6 5 4 3 2 1 0

8. Can you describe specific breakthroughs you have achieved?

   Yes Somewhat No
   6 5 4 3 2 1 0

9. Did you set aside quality time everyday for ValueWorking?

   Yes Somewhat No
   6 5 4 3 2 1 0

10. Do you consider yourself a better ValueWorker now than you did at the beginning of this period?

   Yes Somewhat No
   6 5 4 3 2 1 0

Most of the ValueWorkers you encountered in this chapter would score above 45 on this test. However, regardless of the score you award yourself, your team, or your organization, you can take certain steps to improve or maintain it.

MAGNIFYING VALUEWORK

Like skilled rock climbers working without the safety of ropes, true discoverers keenly focus on their goal, aware of every crevice, cognizant of every possible route, sure of every foot- and handhold. It takes constant vigilance to maintain a high level of discovering and creating breakthroughs. Irrespective of your circumstances, you can improve your ValueWork by following three practical steps: satisfying, exceeding, and pioneering.

Step 1. Satisfying: Match the Needs of Customers, Employees, or Other Stakeholders with the Value That You Create. Measuring how well the value you deliver satisfies the needs of current customers or stakeholders is the starting point. For example, if a customer expects high quality and low cost, a ValueWorker discovers the best way to fulfill that expectation. If a customer wants quick turnaround and mass customization, the ValueWorker focuses on improving turnaround time and providing greater flexibility in customization. Regardless of the specific needs or demands of their customers, Value-Workers strive for a deep understanding of what their customers really want—their true needs. The more detailed and comprehensive your understanding, the more successful your ValueWork will prove. Test marketing, focus groups, customer satisfaction surveys, cultural audits, community opinion polls, and other communications with stakeholders can help you gain the necessary information.

For example, when Microsoft developed the MS-DOS operating system for its client, IBM, the company was working at this stage of ValueWork, discovering new ways to increase the value it delivered to an existing set of customers. Needless to say, the rewards of that one breakthrough for Microsoft have been substantial.

Step 2. Exceeding: Expand Value to Exceed the Current and Future Needs of Customers, Employees, and Other

Stakeholders. The next step consists of anticipating what current customers, employees, or other stakeholders will want or need in the future, then discovering new ways to satisfy those needs. Success at this stage of improvement hinges on developing scenarios of the future. If you can anticipate future breakthroughs, you will be more likely to dedicate resources toward turning those possibilities into reality. Discovery at this stage focuses on enhancing existing products, services, methods, and approaches in ways that will satisfy future needs.

For some time, the 3M Corporation has concentrated its discovery efforts entirely on "adhesives applied to a flat plane," a focus that has continually advanced the ValueWork that 3M people perform by anticipating and meeting their customers' needs in this specific area. Similarly, the *Wall Street Journal* exemplifies second-stage ValueWorking by consistently reporting information that captures current and future business concerns, pushing forward the edge of discovery in the field of business and management.

Step 3. Pioneering: Uncover New Value and New Customers. In the final step, the emphasis shifts to pure discovery. In this, ValueWorkers may find new value for which no current customer or stakeholder exists. If so, the discoverer will quickly move to create a market for the breakthrough. A breakthrough at this stage may or may not arise as a result of a customer need or want. Who could have identified, based on existing customer needs at the time, the demand for CDs, music videos, or interactive software games?

AT&T's Bell Laboratories consistently undertake pure research projects with no specific market or customer in mind. This sort of pursuit uncovers knowledge and new innovations that position the company on the leading edge. Sometimes breakthroughs create entirely new industries. For example, the emergence of the software industry required the establishment of an entirely new set of SIC (Standard Industry Classification) codes to define it.

At this final stage of ValueWorking, there is a risk that a discovery may prove so impractical that the organization cannot translate it into the creation of value. To minimize that risk, a continual assessment of discovery efforts can help set the right direction for those efforts. Ask yourself, "Can I foresee a way to create value if I continue down this path of discovery?" If not, how can you adjust the path of discovery to ensure the ultimate creation of value?

There are no secret formulas for figuring out when your search will pay off or when it won't. You can only keep asking the tough, probing questions while you remain hopeful and confident in your search. This stage of ValueWork makes many companies and workers extremely uncomfortable because it involves so much uncertainty. Trip Hawkins of 3DO showed that a great technological or marketing breakthrough doesn't always guarantee success in the short term. In most cases, discoveries occur before anyone comprehends all their possible applications. However, the future resides in this stage of ValueWork. Many of tomorrow's organizations will provide entirely new services and products. No one can predict with any accuracy what those products or services and their markets will look like, but one sure fact will govern the future: Those workers who pursue discoveries on several fronts simultaneously stand the best chance of inventing a prosperous future for themselves, their teams, and their organizations.

A fascinating example of a company actively embracing all three steps exists at General Magic, an unusual collaboration among competitors: Apple, Sony, AT&T, Motorola, Philips, France Telecom, Fujitsu, Matsushita, and others. To envision a future world in which people use a handheld device to cruise virtually through downtown shops and offices, conducting business, buying goods, and gaining information, much as they would in real life, General Magic has moved beyond stages one and two of ValueWorking and foresees people sitting at home or aboard a plane to Spain, busily sending out "information agents" to book hotel reservations, obtain magazine articles, buy or sell stocks, review new products and services, or perform a myriad of other tasks.

One of General Magic's founders, Bill Atkinson, views the company's objective this way: "Imagine asking you today to stop using the telephone—never place another phone call. That's sobering, because it's probably more important than any other tool that you've got, more important than your personal computer. So here will be the measure of our success: What happens if I ask you ten years from now to stop using your personal communicator? The idea is that you will say, 'This is core to how I live.'"

Obviously, General Magic gazes at far horizons, yet it fully expects its vision to become a reality soon after the year 2000. Assiduous ValueWorkers will use totally new products and services to create whole new industries that only they can imagine today.

ON BECOMING A VALUEWORKER

Many organizations have begun paying more attention to the knowledge creation processes of ValueWork. Skandia Assurance and Financial Services (AFS) has taken impressive steps in that direction. AFS sells annuities, variable life insurance policies, and other savings and insurance instruments from offices in ten countries, including the United States. One of AFS's highest ranking executives, Leif Edvinsson, joined the company in 1991 to assume responsibility for cataloging and evaluating AFS's knowledge creation assets. In other words, he sought to measure the value of discoveries made by individual employees performing ValueWork. Three main principles guided Edvinsson's thinking:

1. The value of knowledge creation assets exceeds the value of balance sheet assets.

2. Knowledge creation assets provide the key to financial results.

3. Managers must differentiate two forms of knowledge creation property, human and structural capital.

Human capital consists of the innovation and discovery an individual makes, but it doesn't create much value unless the organization converts it into structural capital (i.e., unless information systems, knowledge of market channels, and customer relationships and management focus turn individual knowledge or breakthroughs into the property of the group).

As Edvinsson told *Fortune* reporters when he stressed the importance of structural capital: "It doesn't go home at night or quit and hire on with a rival; it puts new ideas to work; and it can be used again and again to create value." *Fortune* further observed, "It can amplify the value of human capital, marshalling the resources of the corporation, customer lists, talent from other departments—to support a new idea. Or it can subtract from human capital, as anyone knows who has watched the whole kludgy apparatus of his company—a rigid budget process, a snail-paced MIS department, a turf-conscious manager—grind genius into gruel."

Translating AFS's human capital into structural capital helped the company take advantage of the trend toward deregulation of insurance and other financial services. In one project, Edvinsson cut about half of the time and money involved in opening an office in a new country by discovering technology and procedures that AFS could transplant to any country. Even though the company will modify its products and services to meet the customer needs in a given country, this core set of capabilities allows for a common support system for offices worldwide.

Reporting regularly on its ValueWork, AFS has pioneered the use of knowledge creation indicators. It groups figures and ratios into three categories: customers, processes, and renewal.

The ratios include such measures as information technology investments as a percentage of total expenses, information technology employees as a percentage of total employees, business development expenses as a percentage of total expenses, production from new products as a percentage of total production, and administrative expenses as a percentage of gross insurance premiums. Not only does AFS use this information internally, but it releases it publicly as proof of the company's strength.

By measuring the ValueWork performed by its employees, AFS has secured its future. Not only does the company encourage discoveries by each and every employee; but it also searches for structural ways to create more value for more people with these discoveries via an ever more streamlined structural capital delivery system.

LESSONS LEARNED

- ✔ ValueWorkers are discoverers, experimenters, and innovators.

- ✔ Constantly searching for breakthroughs will eventually lead to creating breakthroughs.

- ✔ ValueWork advocates consistently discovering and implementing breakthroughs as the key to creating value over the long term.

- ✔ ValueWorkers employ the skills of searching and creating to satisfy current customer needs, exceed future needs, and pioneer new needs and new value.

- ✔ Those who are not natural ValueWorkers can improve their ValueWorking by adopting ValueWork's three stages: satisfying, exceeding, and pioneering.

CHAPTER FIVE

MetaWorkers

"We cannot with integrity deny our responsibility for stewardship of every part of the whole."

M. Scott Peck

A DAY IN THE LIFE OF A METAWORKER

The day begins at 6:00 A.M. for Roz Wilson (a fictional character) with a 30-minute workout on her Soloflex, followed by a brisk shower. From 7:00 A.M. to 7:30 A.M., the family eats breakfast and discusses everything from their respective day's activities to last night's Knicks-Pacers play-off game. Larry, her writer-composer husband, takes their two daughters, 9-year-old Erica and 13-year-old Briana to school at 7:30 A.M. and then drops Roz at the train station for the hour-and-a-half trip from Bridgeport, Connecticut to midtown Manhattan.

Roz Wilson, 41, is executive vice president of Pomeroy Publishing, one of New York's hottest new paperback publishers with annual revenues of 70 million dollars and a five-year growth rate above 20% per anum. Most people at Pomeroy expect Roz to take over as CEO when founder Bernie Goldstein takes the company public in the next year or two.

Since assuming the post of executive vice president three years ago, Roz has used her train ride to and from work for valuable "think time" before she hits the office. She resists the temptation to occupy the commute time by filling in her day planner or talking on the cellular phone with colleagues and agents because she wants to keep her mind focused on broader ideas. Roz opens her laptop, complete with wireless modem, and calls up the Internet to scan the latest thought-provoking articles in her field, hunting for information that might open up new avenues of innovation for Pomeroy. She can also tap into company databases titled Multimedia, Strategic Alliances, Authors, Technology, and Management and Leadership. As ideas occur to her, she records them in her personal journal, dating and filing them for easy access later. "My other brain," as she calls her computer, has become an integral part of her life and her work. This morning, she makes a note to test out some of the idea-generation and concept-outlining software on the market because her present system doesn't quite satisfy her. She wonders if Pomeroy should perhaps consider developing its own publishing-specific ValueWorking software.

When Roz arrives at her office at 605 Third Avenue, she feels refreshed and ready for a morning of PowerWorking. However, before she dives into her hectic schedule, she dicusses the day ahead with her assistant, Kevin, who reviews all of the necessary meetings and activities ahead. Except for emergency or high-priority calls, Kevin aggressively screens Roz's calls and interruptions throughout the morning, so she can complete all her tasks on time.

At lunchtime another phase of Roz's day begins, during which she networks with a major bookseller, a key supplier, a bestselling author, a potential joint-venture partner, or a fellow publisher. After lunch, she continues that phase by returning calls, making new contacts, meeting with staff, working one-on-one with key associates, calling customers, and considering new business partners. She tries to get out of the office in the afternoons as often as possible to meet with key people face to face in their offices or in a quiet spot.

At 5:30 P.M., she leaves for Grand Central Station and her train ride home. Once again, Roz opens her laptop, reviews the day, and ponders all the new ideas that have developed along the way.

The family reunites for dinner around 7:30 P.M. to discuss the day for each: Erica's struggle with Math; Briana's new best friend, Joelle; the new twist in Larry's novella plot; and the anthology of baseball poetry that Pomeroy will publish in the spring. Roz and Larry spend the rest of the evening from 9:00 P.M. to 11:30 P.M. by themselves, conversing about Erica's problems with subtraction, discussing the need to fix a leaky faucet, and watching the 11:00 P.M. news. Sometimes they stay up for Letterman, but not this time. Tonight, they just want to cuddle with each other in bed.

Roz Wilson has entered the Fourth Dimension, where she moves gracefully and effortlessly in and out of the other three dimensions of work, PowerWorking, NetWorking, and Value-Working, throughout her day. She abides by a simple credo:

The MetaWorker's Credo

I constantly remind myself that my work must include three dimensions: doing, developing, and discovering. My success depends on recognizing when and how to emphasize and mix all the dimensions of my work in a way that propels me into the Fourth Dimension.

This credo weaves the benefits of all the dimensions of work—PowerWorking, NetWorking, and ValueWorking—into a seamless fabric that puts joy into every minute of every day. It automatically decreases the chances that overemphasis on any one dimension of work will get in the way of achieving the very best outcomes one can accomplish in one's life and

work. This chapter shows you how you can pursue the fourth
dimension each and every day from now on.

METAWORKING

In June 1976, Marshall Moriarity (not his real name) graduated
with honors from Harvard Business School and within 30 days
began working for a Big 6 accounting firm, Peat Marwick, as
a management consultant. His early assignments ranged from
organizational planning to financial analysis, and he tackled each
with great enthusiasm. His hard work would, he assumed, set
him securely on an eight- to ten-year track to partnership. However, after 18 months with Peat Marwich, he grew disenchanted
with an ever-changing list of clients and decided to accept a
corporate staff position in strategic planning with PepsiCo,
which he enjoyed immensely for a few months. But soon that
job, too, began to frustrate him because he longed to get closer
to the real action. After lobbying for a line position in one of the
company's operating divisions, he eventually won a marketing
management position at Frito-Lay. Moriarity threw himself into
his new assignment with great gusto, and within a few months,
found himself promoted to Director of Marketing for one of
Frito-Lay's product lines. Nine months later, the company trans-
ferred him to Taco Bell, another PepsiCo division, as Senior
Director of Marketing, with a substantial increase in salary. Well
on his way up the ladder at PepsiCo, Moriarity seemed poised
to forge a stellar business career, but one year later, just six
years out of business school, he abruptly quit Taco Bell to start
a sandwich shop in his hometown of Akron, Ohio. Real success,
he had concluded, would come from building an empire of
his own.

Six years of restless searching for his special niche in the
business world convinced Moriarity that his future lay outside
conventional corporate life. "I couldn't stand the structure, the
routine, the dues, and especially the monotony," he told his
wife at the time. "No one cared about anything but bottom-

line results. Most of all, I couldn't stand the narrowness of thinking and shallowness of concern. Everyone worshiped the bottom line, and I just got sick of it."

Over the next six years, Marshall Moriarity built his sandwich business into a five-location operation, but, to his chagrin, he eventually discovered that he didn't enjoy entrepreneurship any more than he did corporate management. Eventually, he found himself looking forward more to his vacations than to the daily pressure at work, and he frequently confided to his wife about his dissatisfaction. "I really don't like going to work every day," he complained. "In fact, I dread it." After a lot of encouragement from his wife, Moriarity finally looked up Jed Kee, an old high school friend and clinical psychologist with a private practice in Cleveland.

As he sits down for his first session with Kee, Moriarity vents his frustrations, then asks Kee, "What's wrong with me?"

Kee, a large man with a calm and reassuring manner, smiles at his friend. "What do *you* think is wrong?"

"I hate working."

Kee laughs. "I've known you for 30 years, Marsh. My guess is you're just misapplying your talent."

"You mean I shouldn't have gone to business school?"

"No. I mean you've got to keep searching."

"For what?"

"Connection. Connection with your work."

"Are you connected?"

"Yes. I love what I'm doing."

"I wish I could say that."

"I know. I think you're suffering from what I call one-dimensionalism. You're so intense about everything you do, and you have felt a need to direct that intensity to your business because you're a Harvard Business School grad, and that's what every good Harvard man does. This is only a guess, my friend, but I think you're preventing yourself from pursuing the real loves of your life."

Moriarity puts his head in his hands. "I don't know where to start. I've been chasing so many rainbows, I feel I've lost my way. Where do I start?"

"You start with that realization. Then we can run you through some preference-aptitude tests, talk about the results, and begin hammering out a plan of action."

Over the next several weeks, Moriarity learns, to his surprise, that his psychological profile places him outside the realm of typical business management. No wonder he has chafed under the constraints of every conventional business situation he has entered. He also discovers that he possesses an unmet need for creative and innovative work, an insight that helps to explain why he has always felt excited at the beginning of a new job, but could never sustain that enthusiasm.

With Kee's help, Marshall Moriarity begins identifying things he would love to do, but never took time to explore, such as more serious reading, poetry-writing, oil painting, pottery, bird watching, landscape design, and archaeology. The list surprises Marshall but not Kee, who explains, "Many business people force themselves to endure a narrowly focused work life. They direct their energies toward getting results in their work and find real pleasure only in weekend recreation and occasional extended vacations or retreats. You need to pursue a broader range of interests, but, unfortunately, most of those interests lie outside the traditional field of management and business. Most people come to accept their dissatisfactions. You haven't."

As Kee and Moriarity work out a plan of action, they discuss the reality that most people live a one-dimensional life or, at best, two-dimensional lives based on the faulty assumption that life requires choosing one path over another.

"In reality," observes Kee, "the people who enjoy the best mental health and experience the greatest sense of joy actively cultivate multiple dimensions of their lives. They are what we psychologists call whole, balanced, well-rounded people. They work hard, but they gain greater fulfillment than a paycheck or a fancy title."

Moriarity agrees. "I've been kidding myself that the more focused I am, the happier I will be."

"Sure. You've been deploying yourself as a corporate resource, but life is so much more than that. If business organizations only took a broader view of their employees, instead of seeing them solely as a means to an end, they would get better results. More well-rounded people, those who have explored and developed the full range of their personalities, always accomplish more in their chosen work. Like most people, you naturally incline toward such integration and balance, and you may have solved this problem sooner or later, with or without my help. Maybe I've accelerated the process, but the answer has come, not from the outside, but from within yourself."

In the months that follow, Moriarity sells his chain of sandwich outlets and moves his family to Santa Fe, New Mexico, where he opens a pottery gallery and studio. Committed to living a multidimensional life, Moriarity works hard at building his new business four hours a day from noon to 4:00 P.M. In the mornings he reads voraciously, writes poetry, and spends time helping his wife get their children off to school. In the evenings, he serves on a local arts council, volunteers at a nearby homeless shelter, and with his wife, reads to their two children and teaches them to throw pots. After eight years in Santa Fe, Marshall Moriarity describes his life as full, balanced, and delightful. He loves his work. He has expanded his pottery gallery and studio to three locations, opened a coffee shop bookstore, published a book of poetry, designed a new potter's wheel, established an enduring bond with his wife and children, and has recently become chairman of the Santa Fe Arts Council. In 1996, Marshall Moriarity finally finds his life worth living.

Without fully understanding the notion, Moriarity learned how to perform MetaWork by moving outside the one-dimensional focus of his earlier career. A natural NetWorker, who spent most of his time PowerWorking, he had not, in his early business career, paid enough attention to ValueWorking. While natural PowerWorkers can endure single-dimensional work experiences better than natural NetWorkers or Value-Workers, few can find the fulfillment and peace that Moriarity found when he combined all three dimensions to achieve the fourth dimension—MetaWork. MetaWorkers move comfortably in the three dimensions of work, and by doing so, enter the fourth dimension and transcend to a higher level of human performance.

WORKING COMFORTABLY IN THE THREE DIMENSIONS

How do people achieve the fourth dimension? What tangible traits do they exhibit? It's not easy, of course, to concretely describe a dimension of life and work characterized by such words as "joy," "fulfillment," and "love." It defies a simple checklist of clear-cut steps because such a mechanical approach constricts thinking and fosters a false sense of security. Any "cookbook" method stifles the individual's search for his or her own true calling. Entering the fourth dimension requires a deep understanding of one's own nature, aptitudes, and preferences, as well as a detailed awareness of the three dimensions of work. Then, through a combination of self-understanding, gut feelings, and practical sensing, the MetaWorker can set about achieving a sort of joy that eludes so many in our hectic work-a-day world. MetaWorkers don't measure their worth only in terms of salary increases and bonuses, because they value their true achievements, not just the goals set forth in job descriptions, but accomplishments that shape their lives and define their beings. MetaWorkers weave their commitments to results, competence, and breakthroughs into a colorful tapestry of PowerWork, NetWork, and ValueWork. With this in mind, consider Table 5.1, which shows how PowerWorking, NetWorking, and ValueWorking can be woven together to create the fourth dimension.

By constantly monitoring achievement in these three dimensions, anyone can gain greater control over his or her destiny. The following guidelines and examples give you a final review before asking the ultimate question: "Am I a MetaWorker?"

THE FIRST DIMENSION: POWERWORKING

PowerWorkers strive for a sense of control—control over their environment, control over what goes on during the day, and control over their resources. They win respect from others for the results they achieve.

Table 5.1.   The fourth dimension: working in all three dimensions

	My Work	Response From Others	My Experience
PowerWork	• Manage costs • Deploy resources • Focus on activities, priorities, systems, and practices	• Recognition for usefulness, no waste, and getting the job done	• Doing • Control • Results
NetWork	• Develop talents and capabilities • Cultivate supportive relationships • Establish partnerships	• Gratitude for contribution, skills, and participation	• Developing • Influence • Competence
ValueWork	• Meet customer and stakeholder needs • Anticipate future needs • Discover breakthroughs	• Praise for knowledge, insight, and innovation	• Discovering • Value • Breakthroughs

Ralene Childs serves as the director of a Redevelopment Agency (RDA) for a midsize urban city. RDA is an organization set up to rehabilitate and redevelop areas of the city that have deteriorated to the point where they no longer provide adequate housing or employment. The agency seeks to restore economic vitality to these areas by facilitating and encouraging the return of tenants and business owners.

Ralene Childs exemplifies the PowerWorker. During her years of service as the director, she has implemented a number of procedures and processes that encourage efficiency and effectiveness throughout her operations. She has inaugurated detailed cash projections and construction budgets for each renovation her office has undertaken. Her staff analyzes the market potential for each piece of property to determine in advance the size of the investment the city should put toward its redevelopment. She measures success by the number of square feet her office returns to use through renovation, reporting and tracking such measurements regularly. In addition, Childs compares her efforts to those in similar cities and reports the comparisons to the City Council and the RDA board of directors.

Entering her office, a visitor immediately sees that she has gained a lot of formal recognition for her work. On the wall certificates presented to her by the City Council, the League of Women Voters, and others for her wise use of public funds, her conservative mangement style, and her good business sense are hung. Childs herself exudes a sense of confidence derived from knowing she's doing good work. Unafraid to field tough questions that the media or others may ask regarding her budget or use of funds, she is completely comfortable with the scrutiny associated with working in the public sector. She's always in control because she possesses the facts and knows both what her office accomplishes and how its accomplishments compare to those of similar agencies. Ralene Childs knows she's a Power-Worker from what she accomplishes, from the responses of others, and from what she personally experiences working in the first dimension.

The Second Dimension: NetWorking

Never standing on the sidelines as casual observers, NetWorkers continually expand their influence and involve themselves ever more deeply in their relationships. Competence and common purpose among the team or group increase both their personal satisfaction and their tangible accomplishments.

Charles Kimball works as a graphic designer in the children's division of a company that publishes monthly magazines for various age groups, including teenagers and adults. Given the tremendous technological changes in the graphic design field, Charles has striven to stay abreast of the latest developments, investing his own money in the latest computer equipment and software in order to sharpen the skills that he believes he needs to succeed in his profession.

During discussions with the design team responsible for the adult magazine, Kimball saw how his division could benefit enormously from the latest software tools that specify and communicate color pigmentation commands to the company's sophisticated state-of-the-art color printers. Although this work fell outside his own area of direct responsibility, Kimball gladly offered his knowledge and expertise to the team.

In essence, he joined the other team temporarily, working for a brief but intense period of time on their project. As a team member, he not only brought his own considerable technological skills to bear on crucial design considerations, but he also learned from his new teammates. They had, he discovered, already solved some of the sophisticated color screening problems that he would soon face.

At the end of the project, the team took Charles to lunch and presented him with the framed cover of the magazine he had helped to redesign. Later, other ad hoc team opportunities arose in which everyone involved both shared and gained new skills. Everybody won.

As a NetWorker, Kimball continually develops his own talents and expands his relationships, contributing wherever he can to gradually increase the sphere of his influence.

The Third Dimension: ValueWorking

Inhabiting the realm of the imagination, ValueWorkers attain a deep sense of self-worth and receive great recognition from others for their creations. Often described as lucky or gifted or always "in the right place at the right time," they, nevertheless, accomplish their breakthroughs because they never stop searching for ways to create more value.

Back in the early 1950s, at the dawn of the fast-food explosion, the Maddox family opened a traditional family-style restaurant and set about discovering how they could survive the new trend. The new drive-in chains seemed to be opening a new outlet every day as increasing numbers of Americans hungered for quick service and inexpensive food even at the cost of quality. The Maddoxes worried that their fledgling restaurant might not fare well in this environment because it took their cooks as long as 20 minutes to prepare a customer meal. With no drive-through service, their customers had to come into a cabin-styled building and sit at a counter or in a small booth.

For months the family considered a variety of ways to counter the fast-food competition, all the while watching their business decline as customers opted for quicker service and more convenience than their traditional restaurant could provide. After a lot of soul searching, the family decided to open an outdoor drive-in next to their existing facility. However, they chose not to design the new operation as a typical drive-in with car hops running back and forth between customers' cars and the order window. Instead, they went one step further toward providing value to their customers.

Accepting the fact that customers demanded speed and would not tolerate even the shortest delay, the Maddox's automated the ordering and delivery of their food with an elaborate, chain-driven carousel that delivered small Plexiglas containers to customers' cars. These containers, hanging on small, chain-like gondolas, traveled to the very end of the drive-in lanes where car hops took orders for food, inserted them into the empty containers, and sent them on their way to the kitchen. Then as cooks filled the orders, the food went into the containers and began the journey out to the eager customers. Children delighted in watching the containers drift from their cars to the kitchen and back again.

The Maddox family did not just settle for meeting their customers' expectations, but worked to exceed them by offering more value via an inventive and entertaining device. The quality of their food, the excitement of their system, and the speed of their service quickly attracted customers. Business boomed, and both the restaurant and drive-in rang up record business.

Through ValueWork, the Maddox family has continually discovered new ways to satisfy their customers and, in the process, increased the number of regular patrons year after year. Since 1950, the Maddox restaurant has expanded, remodeled, and redirected its focus several times to create new and better value for its customers. Today, it remains a thriving concern.

THE FOURTH DIMENSION: METAWORKING

Ralene Childs, Charles Kimball, and the Maddox family all accomplished a lot in the work dimensions in which they were most comfortable. By doing so, each garnered both recognition and personal satisfaction while moving closer to the threshold of the fourth dimension. Childs could now use NetWorking and ValueWorking to build stronger relationships with area businesses and neighboring cities and communities, as well as target strategic developments offering the greatest value to her city. Kimball could turn to PowerWorking and ValueWorking to increase the efficiency and effectiveness of his response to a growing number of opportunities, as well as carefully select the projects offering him and the company the greatest potential benefits. The Maddox family could rely on PowerWorking and NetWorking to exploit their position by licensing or selling their innovations to others, as well as by applying their creative vision to other related businesses through acquisitions or strategic partnerships.

Can these workers take the next step to become MetaWorkers? Can you?

"AM I A METAWORKER?"

You might begin to answer this question, by comprehensively assessing your current levels of work in the three dimensions. In the three previous chapters, you considered a series of assessment questions designed to help you determine the degree to which you perform as a PowerWorker, NetWorker, or ValueWorker. Now, you can monitor your ability to combine the three dimensions and move into the fourth dimension by using the MetaWork Journal (Figure 5.1) on a daily, weekly, or monthly basis.

Keep two thoughts in mind as you use this tool. First, the MetaWork Journal is a monitoring tool for reviewing and evaluating your efforts in each work dimension. Second, the MetaWork Journal gives you the opportunity to record needed adjustments in work dimension emphasis or mix. MetaWorking is a process, not a product, one that requires continual monitoring and adjustment.

As Ralene Childs, Charles Kimball, and the Maddox family learned, strength in one dimension can accomplish a lot, but weaknesses in the other dimensions can compromise results, competence, and breakthroughs. MetaWorkers grasp the strengths and weaknesses associated with each of the three dimensions of work, well aware that relying on the strengths of only one or two dimensions can prevent them from realizing their ultimate goals. The satisfaction and rewards that come from working well in one of the dimensions can, in fact, compel a worker to stay in that dimension. When people reach their comfort zones and feel satisfied with their achievements in a single dimension, they miss the opportunities for greater achievement that come from working in all three dimensions and thus moving into the fourth. The following table highlights

Figure 5.1. MetaWork Journal: Monitoring.

	Increasing Results	Improving Competence	Achieving Breakthroughs
POWERWORK	**Measure:** Were you able to Measure the progress and outcomes of your performance?	**Benchmark:** Did you Benchmark the best practices of others?	**Redesign:** Have you started Redesigning work process to dramatically increase output?
	☐ Need Improvement ☐ Satisfactory ☐ Outstanding	☐ Need Improvement ☐ Satisfactory ☐ Outstanding	☐ Need Improvement ☐ Satisfactory ☐ Outstanding
NETWORK	**Select:** Have you Selected the right people and skills for success?	**Cultivate:** Are you Cultivating the best talents and relationships for the future?	**Partner:** Did you explore any new Partnerships with individuals or organizations to substantially improve capabilities?
	☐ Need Improvement ☐ Satisfactory ☐ Outstanding	☐ Need Improvement ☐ Satisfactory ☐ Outstanding	☐ Need Improvement ☐ Satisfactory ☐ Outstanding
VALUEWORK	**Satisfy:** Did you Satisfy existing customer/ stakeholder needs?	**Exceed:** Are you working to Exceed current customer/ stakeholder expectations of worth and value?	**Pioneer:** Have you begun pioneering revolutionary approaches, products, or services that create significant new value for customers/ stakeholders?
	☐ Need Improvement ☐ Satisfactory ☐ Outstanding	☐ Need Improvement ☐ Satisfactory ☐ Outstanding	☐ Need Improvement ☐ Satisfactory ☐ Outstanding

Figure 5.1. (continued)   MetaWork Journal: Adjustments.

Powerwork

Time spent   Today's %   Tomorrow's %

Today's Outcomes

Tomorrow's Adjustments

Network

Time spent   Today's %   Tomorrow's %

Today's Outcomes

Tomorrow's Adjustments

Valuework

Time spent   Today's %   Tomorrow's %

Today's Outcomes

Tomorrow's Adjustments

the weaknesses of single-dimension work and provides a cautionary note (Table 5.2).

Remember that overcoming the weaknesses of a single work dimension can improve your MetaWorking, but it will take courage, humility, and vision to affect that transformation.

THE PRINCIPLES OF METAWORKING

We have purposefully avoided reducing the MetaWork system to a formula or a detailed set of steps, because the paths to MetaWork vary from person to person, as people embark on individual quests shaped by their own unique backgrounds, personalities, capabilities and desires. However, three essential principles govern progress on the path to MetaWorking and characterize the fundamental attitude of a true MetaWorker.

PRINCIPLE 1. RESIST THE NATURAL INCLINATION TO WORK SOLELY IN YOUR MOST COMFORTABLE DIMENSION

Like most people, you probably are most comfortable in one of the first three dimensions of work. That natural ability has shaped who you are, the talents you possess, your education, your past work experiences, your goals and, to some extent, the dimension of work on which you have most relied in the past to accomplish your goals. Given this inclination, you probably have developed a preference for PowerWorking, NetWorking, or ValueWorking, and, over time, you have become more confident and secure working in that dimension.

Although this natural tendency may have served you well in the past, it could prevent you from entering or mastering the other dimensions of work that will open up the fourth dimension for you. As the pressures of work increase and demands become more intense, instead of pushing yourself into another dimension or the final dimension, you may fall back into an old reliable

Table 5.2. Weaknesses of single-dimension work

Dimension	Weaknesses	Caution
PowerWork	• Ignoring or denying the value of NetWork and ValueWork • Becoming too entrenched in PowerWork • Discounting the talent of natural NetWorkers and ValueWorkers • Seeing NetWork and ValueWork as overly simple or as not significant	PowerWorkers must resist the temptation to disregard the other two dimensions. They must look beyond the short-term "rewards" they receive by doing PowerWork and focus on the longer term.
NetWork	• Relying excessively on the skill of bringing PowerWorkers and ValueWorkers together • Overemphasizing their contribution • Loosing "credibility" by not "Doing" or "Discovering" • Believing they have done their part by simply bringing the talent together	NetWorkers generally feel optimistic because they see such great potential in others. They must recognize that workers in the other dimensions often view their work as less significant and easy to accomplish. This can lead to alienation and resentment within a group. NetWorkers must make a larger contribution by working in the other dimensions as well.
ValueWork	• Believing that only this dimension of work really matters • Appearing arrogant • Feeling that PowerWork and NetWork will naturally fall in place • Becoming detached and isolated • Providing roadblocks to NetWorking	ValueWorkers must recognize that their discoveries create little value without PowerWorking and NetWorking. They must welcome NetWorking and avoid the arrogance that frustrates and alienates PowerWorkers.

pattern that promises the most immediate results. In doing so, you may experience a temporary sense of accomplishment, but unless you can move freely into the most appropriate dimension for your circumstances, you will fail to reap the rewards of that optimum dimension. Even if your are a natural ValueWorker who wants to remain primarily focused on that dimension of work, appropriate and timely PowerWorking or NetWorking can improve your ValueWorking.

Complacency in one dimension can create a vicious cycle. As the desired long-term outcome recedes, frustration increases. Instead of tapping the benefits of the other work dimensions, frustrated people entrench themselves in comfortable patterns, bury their heads, or put on their blinders as they stiffen their resolve to tough it out and stay the course. However, during those occasional moments of forced or chosen awakening when such people raise their heads and take off their blinders, they see themselves far from their goals, off track, or lost. At such moments they begin to hear the criticism. Some even listen.

Wesley Faulkner (a fictitious name), the CEO of AlphaOmega (also disguised), one of the fastest-growing high-technology companies in the United States, felt wonderful when *Fortune* and *Inc.* magazines recognized his company as an "up and comer," "a company poised for even more incredible growth in the future." From every outsider's point of view, this company seemed destined to rack up an impressive record well into the next century.

Six years ago, when Faulkner took over, he found a company completely "out of control." Sales hovered around ten million dollars annually; the organization lacked sound financial controls; middle managers could spend money without any review; budgets did not exist; and the firm used only crude measures to gauge financial performance. A natural PowerWorker, Faulkner seemed perfect for the job of turning this company around. His impressive record in the financial services industry, in which he had gotten several companies under control, indicated that he could bring to AlphaOmega the efficiency and effectiveness the firm so desperately needed.

Right off the bat, he put in place a tight financial approval process. No one could write a check without Faulkner's signature, and no one could incur obligations over $500 unless Faulkner formally approved. He firmly took into his own hands the authority to approve all projects, all future programs, and all hiring. Of course, this did not sit well with managers accustomed to almost total freedom. Even the groundskeeper complained, "Faulkner would tell me how to cut the lawn. One day he called me up and told me that I wasn't watering the lawn enough. He said the golf course behind his house was watered every day. I had to put a stack of agronomy books on his desk to convince him that different soils require different watering cycles."

Faulkner's PowerWork quickly began to stabilize Alpha-Omega. The board of directors and outside investors applauded and encouraged every move he made. As a result of his actions, the company, with more than 1,300 employees in six separate departments, has now grown to a point where annual sales exceed $200 million.

That's the good news. What's the bad news? Although many of Faulkner's early procedures have become firmly entrenched in the organization, AlphaOmega has not expanded or innovated beyond its original line of computer and peripheral products. At this point, the company desperately needs to create new products and pursue new markets if it is to stay on the competitive edge of its industry, but Faulkner refuses to bestow the freedom necessary for the company to do so. He continues to insist on the same degree of control, the same centralization of power, and the same pursuit of greater efficiency that won the admiration of the board and the business press. Those fans might view the company's future differently if they knew how many purchase orders for needed equipment get delayed for weeks because Faulkner simply can't get to them all, or how the hiring of key personnel sometimes takes two months because of all the required approvals. The innovation and discovery that the company should be making by shifting its emphasis to ValueWork cannot come about if Faulkner insists on controlling every decision. As so often happens, his personal skills, taken to the extreme, have become a liability.

Even the company's limited attempt to develop NetWork by forming alliances with key partners has ground to a halt because Faulkner has refused to consider any joint-venture projects unless the partners agree to a full takeover and merger. As a result, many interested strategic partners, whose talents would nicely complement those of AlphaOmega, have gone elsewhere.

Under some pressure from the board and outside investors to change his approach, Faulkner has responded by stiffening his resolve to continue his course. His focus on PowerWork alone, at the expense of NetWork and ValueWork, will likely force the board eventually to replace him.

PRINCIPLE 2. ALLY WITH OTHERS WHOSE MOST DOMINANT WORK DIMENSIONS DIFFER FROM YOUR OWN

Mastering all three dimensions of work takes time, of course, and while you're striving to enter the fourth dimension, you can support your efforts and gain valuable role models by combining your own work preferences with those of others. In approaching any task, use your understanding of your own capabilities and weaknesses to identify where you need support. PowerWorkers can seek out NetWorkers and ValueWorkers, and vice versa, thereby creating MetaWork conditions in a team or organization. Entrepreneurs, too, can benefit from this principle by forming complementary alliances with others.

Application of this principle requires a full understanding of your own and potential teammates' strengths and abilities, as well as a willingness to see others as crucial to your own success. "Protecting your own turf" must give way to "protecting your own (your team's, your organization's) ultimate success." When this occurs, the inclination to associate or work only with "kindred spirits," those who function best in the same dimension as yourself, diminishes. Instead of looking for collaborators or loyal followers, look for teammates who together can achieve the wholeness of the fourth dimension.

Sharon Deane knows how to create value, and her discovery skills serve her well in her work as an expert witness. Deane can take a highly complex business lawsuit and plow through the details of the numbers, decipher endless piles of financial documents, and pinpoint the most significant issue on which the whole case rests. She applies her unique talent to build a case either for or against that issue, loading all the relevant information into her computer-like mind, and then calmly fielding tough questions on the witness stand. Under intense interrogation, she crystallizes the issues down to statements the jury and judge can understand, making the most complex and baffling situation seem clear and simple.

Deane possesses one other skill: She knows that she is not a natural NetWorker or PowerWorker. Although she has tried to expand her accomplishment in these other two dimensions, she recognizes that mastery of them will take years of concentrated effort. Early in her career, she tried but failed to create her own expert witness consulting business because she was a poor NetWorker. Uncomfortable at marketing herself, she does not relate well to groups and grows impatient with the "dance" of getting acquainted with prospective clients.

She also recognizes her deficiencies in the PowerWorking dimension. Although she loves to discover the key elements of a case and will spend day and night unraveling the mystery, like Sherlock Holmes, she quickly loses interest once she has cracked the case. As a result, she does not document her findings painstakingly enough, lets paper pile up on her desk and in her briefcase, and generally lacks the discipline to record all the details of her discovery. Armed with this knowledge, she eventually joined forces with a NetWorker and a PowerWorker.

"The best thing I ever did was go into business with Trish Bingham and Kirk Shaw," says Deane. "Trish is a great Net-Worker. She's a natural at meeting people, forging relationships, and presenting my skills in a way that attracts business. Kirk helps make sense of what I've done, writing it all down, putting it in files, and accurately documenting what I do."

Bingham and Shaw make excellent matches for Deane. Bingham's NetWorking skills have not only positioned the company in its market and stimulated much of its growth, but her crucial skills have also fostered the development of key alliances with other small consulting businesses. When large consulting projects come along, Bingham manages to get a portion of the business by joint venturing Deane's talents with those of other firms. Shaw's PowerWorking discipline has brought to the business all of the procedures and systems that once frustrated Deane. His work has greatly improved the efficiency and credibility of the office and has won the confidence of an increasing number of steady clients.

"The hardest part for me," says Deane, "was realizing early on that I needed help in these other dimensions. I had a tendency to think that my intellect would carry me through. My pride took a beating when I realized that wasn't true. While it was a humbling experience, it has been absolutely exhilarating to see what we can accomplish together."

PRINCIPLE 3. STRIVE TO INCREASE THE METAWORKING OF OTHERS

Assisting others to become better MetaWorkers not only improves the organization and the team, but it also develops the individual. Unfortunately, too many organizations still delight in pitting workers against one another in the name of "productive competition." After all, they claim, people must compete fiercely for the few top jobs, beating the other person to get there. Too many executives and managers today pay too little attention to their equals and their subordinates as they focus all their attention on winning the support of those above them.

MetaWorking requires a radically different approach. As individuals work with others to increase their ability to MetaWork, they also learn from others new ways to PowerWork, new ways to NetWork, and new ways to ValueWork. In the new world of MetaWorking, traditional organizational hierarchies, structures, and control systems must give way to fields of work where doing, developing, and discovering occur. Your own success depends not only on the successes of others, but it also hinges on ensuring that others succeed.

At the age of 75, Wesley Paul still works actively and successfully as a real estate salesman. Over the years, his career has spanned a wide range of jobs and professions. He started as a building maintenance supervisor for the local school district, then managed a B.F. Goodrich retail store during the boom years of the 1950s, from which he moved on to run his own retail home furnishing business for many years, until he sold it and took a position as manager of a nonprofit urban renewal organization. Most recently, he joined an old friend in the real estate business.

Throughout all of these work experiences Paul has always operated according to the principle that his personal success would come from helping those around him to grow and prosper. Thus, he constantly searched for ways to help others become the best they could be. Although never expecting any tangible payback, he assumed that helping his associates would somehow benefit him personally in the long run. "I have always tried to help others consider how they could do their work better," Paul reminisces. "I've tried to help them think of new ways of accomplishing things and developing the best within them. And I always tried to help them become more well-rounded, able to see the other's point of view."

Struggling through the Great Depression years, Paul, like so many of his generation, developed a strong sense of PowerWork. "We simply had to learn how to do things for less. There wasn't much of anything around," he recalls. "When managing the Goodrich store, it was sort of a game to see who could install a set of tires in the least amount of time. I kept a chart up on the wall and tracked the times of each of the repairmen. We had a lot of fun with that."

With a keen eye for talent, Paul has tried to develop the abilities of those around him. Many of his protegés have become remarkably successful in their own fields. As Dave Hardman, senior manager for a national retail merchandising chain remembers, "It was Wesley Paul who first thought I could manage others. I was pretty young at the time, but he felt that I could manage the electronics department of his store. He saw in me things that I didn't see in myself. He worked with me, developed my skills and spent extra time with me. To this day, I still apply the advice I received from him because it's made me a better person. There's a unique wholeness to Paul that seems to rub off on others."

Through his efforts, Wesley Paul has discovered the great benefits that derive from helping others to become MetaWorkers. "Many of my employees, the ones I worked with most, have become my best customers over the years," he concludes. "My partner today is a man who worked for me many years ago. Now he seeks me out and gives me an opportunity to keep myself involved in something meaningful, even at my age."

Paul believes that every investment he has made to increase the work abilities of others has not only increased their fulfillment, but has made his own life richer and more rewarding.

ON TRANSFORMING YOURSELF INTO A METAWORKER

You can use these three principles to marshal two forces that all people must harness as they attempt to transform themselves into MetaWorkers: (1) the power of wholeness that comes with working in all three dimensions, and (2) the power that understanding your work dimension strength lends to any team or organization. These two forces combine harmoniously, one pushing you toward wholeness, balance, and breadth, the other toward specialization, focus, and depth. MetaWork constantly blends these two forces. As an individual, you will achieve greater results, fulfillment, meaning, wholeness, and joy if you strive toward the fourth dimension. As a team or organization member, your group will achieve more by tapping, developing, and integrating the discipline, talents, and knowledge of each member for the greatest benefit of the entire group.

The MetaWork system enables you to recognize the need to become both a specialist and a generalist. Sadly, modern managerial traditions too often force organizations and teams to stress only the specialist role because doing so seemingly generates greater efficiency and effectiveness. Such an emphasis promotes PowerWork at the expense of NetWork and Value-Work, and it explains why so many people today work more but enjoy it less. If continued, this course, which sacrifices the future for the present, will only burn out employees, something that U.S. companies have been doing far too long. MetaWorking can reverse this damaging trend.

The new world of work requires a new life pattern without boundaries to progress and development. No matter what your current work preferences or experiences are, you can transform yourself into a MetaWorker. It will take time and effort, but you can get there before you turn 65. If you're already past 65, it's not too late to start on the path because it's not just a function of years, but of awareness and growth. For some, it may take a few years. For others it may never completely come, but the striving alone brings a certain fulfillment. Transformation into the fourth dimension is not a project with a beginning, middle, and end; it's a process, a neverending journey of self-discovery and application. You never reach a final destination, but keep spiraling higher and higher in your quest for greater achievement, fulfillment, and contribution. The process does not depend on your age, your background, or your present preferences, but on your willingness to look hard at yourself, your work, and your patterns of accomplishment. If you stay on the path spiraling upward, you will perform more powerful, meaningful, and valuable work.

This enlightened pattern of life has always appeared in the most wise, seasoned, and successful leaders who have managed to shift from specialization and narrowness to generalization and breadth at just the right time in their careers to facilitate their continued rise in the organization. Today, with the death of traditional jobs and hierarchical structures, every worker must think, feel, and act more like a CEO, managing their careers as thriving small businesses, developing their strengths, and then overcoming their weaknesses. The idea of the learning organization that pushes for constant improvement and continuous lifelong education for the individual serves as the primary engine of MetaWork.

MetaWorking provides the framework for development and helps you meld the two transformational forces of wholeness and focus in the right proportions and at the right times in your push toward superachievement, maximum fulfillment, and enduring joy. The next three chapters show you, regardless of your stage of life, how to begin unleashing the power of Meta-Work in your everyday life.

THE TENETS OF METAWORK

1. Work is a fundamental element of my life, an activity essential to all aspects of my life, whether in my profession, my family, my community, or my personal moments.

2. Improving how I work will improve all other aspects of my life.

3. Work is not just a means to an end, but an end in and of itself. My work can and should fulfill and satisfy me at the deepest levels.

4. I possess unique capabilities and talents from which I can create something of lasting value.

5. The responsibility to improve how I work rests first and foremost in my own hands.

6. Work occurs in three basic dimensions: doing, developing, and discovering.

7. The key to success in any endeavor lies in recognizing when and how to emphasize and mix the three dimensions of work, thereby enabling me to enter the Fourth Dimension.

8. Leaders, managers, teams, and organizations that encourage work in all three dimensions and move into the Fourth Dimension of MetaWork will become Super-Achievers and create the "best in world" performance of the future.

CHAPTER SIX

Personal Transformations

> "It is not enough to understand what we ought to be,
> unless we know what we are; and we do not understand
> what we are, unless we know what we ought to be."
>
> *T.S. Eliot*

A METAWORK EXERCISE FOR TRANSFORMING INDIVIDUAL PERFORMANCE

Imagine yourself as John Meyers, a 43-year-old manager of one of DuPont's many chemical additives divisions. It's seven o'clock on a bleak December Friday evening, and you are sitting at your desk staring at an interoffice memo. Everyone else went home long ago, and although you, too, should be home with your wife and children, you cannot pull yourself away from this single page of company stationery that drove a knife into your heart a mere two hours earlier. One sentence leaps out from the rest: "We are pleased to announce the promotion of Sarah Watkins to the position of Vice President of Operations." Your pain has nothing to do with Sarah, herself. She's an extremely capable and highly deserving colleague. You like and respect her very much. In fact, you see no problem working for Sarah.

Yet you cannot control your resentment that she, not you, has won this position. Angrily you shove the memo into a desk drawer and stare out the window at the city street lights in the distance.

"I've spent the last fifteen years of my career with this company," you think, recalling how you started at the chemical processing plant as a young engineer. Assigned to plant operations, you relished the opportunity to apply your education at a world-class company. DuPont had thrived for over a century and had provided so many before you with secure and well-paid careers that you had simply assumed it would turn out the same for you. Over the years, you attended many parties and banquets honoring retiring managers and employees, and you marveled at their pensions, stock options, and other retirement benefits garnered from years of service at DuPont. On such occasions, you told yourself, "All I have to do is keep working hard and the same thing will happen to me."

The memo about Sarah Watkins' promotion has hit you hard because it so clearly confirms a feeling that has gradually taken hold of you during the past two years as you have begun to feel your career slipping away from you. The slide started subtly at first, as you found yourself excluded from a few key meetings, not included on some key projects. Now, finally, you have been overlooked for a key promotion. "This job should have been mine," you think. "I deserved it. I earned it." Your fist strikes the window frame, jiggling the reflection of lights on the glass.

You know that your family has felt it, too. At home, you've grown distant from your wife, Deborah, and you've reacted to the adolescent problems of young Bill and Jenny with increasing impatience. Family dinner conversations have turned into petty arguments about water spots on the silverware, and Deborah has begun withdrawing from you, perhaps sensing your frustration at work, but reluctant to confront you about your preoccupation. "I can't confide in her," you think. "She doesn't need this burden. And what would I say? I don't even know what's happening myself. Worse, I don't have the slightest idea what to do about it." You peer deep into the darkness of the night, pondering your predicament and searching for some way out of it.

Like John Meyers, thousands of people face a similar dilemma every day. A once-promising career with a good company reaches a certain plateau where feelings of optimism and confidence give way to anxiety, worry, frustration, and, in the end, a sense that somehow this challenge must be conquered. Put yourself in the situation with John Meyers. Help him decide what to do, develop, or discover. By helping him make choices, and by vicariously living with him through the implications of those choices, you can practice MetaWorking before you apply it in your own work.

Although you remain somewhat baffled by your lack of career progress for the past two years, you realize that you must understand yourself more fully before you can figure a way out of this maze. To better understand yourself, you must set aside your negative feelings and begin a careful assessment of your life, your skills, and your dominant work dimension. The following Dominant Work Preference Indicator (Figure 6.1) provides a first step toward that goal. You answer the questions as John Meyers would to assess your natural work preferences and orientations.

If you were John Meyers, the results would indicate that you tend to do PowerWork (Figure 6.2). With PowerWorking as your dominant work dimension, you should naturally wonder whether you should emphasize this dimension more to build on your natural strength, or focus more on one of the other dimensions to broaden your capabilities. Your secondary preference of NetWorking could prove to be the easiest and fastest road to expanding your capabilities, but your greatest weakness lies in ValueWorking, a weakness that may explain your failure to win that key promotion. As you grapple with the possibilities, you must decide on three possible career enhancing options:

Option A: Build on your PowerWorking strength

Option B: Improve your NetWorking capability

Option C: Overcome your weakness in ValueWorking

Figure 6.1. Dominant work preferences indicator.

Circle the answer that appeals to you most or describes you best.

Name: John Meyers

Date: December 16, 1995

1. In a group setting, I enjoy
   a. solving immediate problems.
   b. learning about what others think.
   c. discussing new approaches and methods.

2. I get along best with
   a. scientific people.
   b. realistic people.
   c. artistic people.

3. I am viewed by others as
   a. persuasive.
   b. visionary.
   c. practical.

4. I prefer planning that is based on
   a. facts.
   b. values.
   c. logic.

5. I think about business strategy in terms of
   a. a clear vision.
   b. a detailed plan.
   c. an orchestration of talent.

6. In communicating with others in the organization, I am usually
   a. empathetic.
   b. knowledgeable.
   c. factual.

7. In the midst of a chaotic situation, I strive to
   a. get organized.
   b. remain flexible.
   c. search for a new path.

8. I get most excited about
   a. ideas and principles.
   b. things and events.
   c. relationships and people.

9. I take pride in
   a. looking at things differently.
   b. facilitating change.
   c. being realistic.

10. I look on the mistakes of others with
    a. judgment.
    b. understanding.
    c. tolerance.

11. In my personal life, I search for
    a. truth.
    b. good works.
    c. meaning.

12. I take pride in being
    a. a feeling person.
    b. a thinking person.
    c. a doing person.

13. When evaluating business, I like to think in terms of
    a. daily realities.
    b. human potential.
    c. technological possibilities.

14. I prefer change that is
    a. ingenious and sweeping.
    b. incremental and step-by-step.
    c. continuous and challenging.

15. I am most likely to
    a. keep and develop an employee who is delivering unacceptable performance.
    b. terminate an employee for unacceptable performance.
    c. ask for assistance from corporate human resources.

16. After receiving information, I come to conclusions by
    a. evaluating the details.
    b. looking for insights.
    c. identifying the principles involved.

17. In business, I prefer understanding
    a. the economic logic before addressing operating details.
    b. the operating details before worrying about the full picture.
    c. the people issues before dealing with any operating details.

Figure 6.1. *(Continued)*

18. I work to enhance organizational
    capabilities by
    (a.) introducing new approaches.
    b. conceiving of breakthrough
       approaches.
    c. improving existing approaches.
19. I attempt to improve results from
    people by
    a. giving them clear instructions.
    (b.) applauding their strivings.
    c. pointing out their failings.
20. I believe that the best way to
    prepare for the future is to
    a. boldly invent tomorrow.
    b. find success today.
    (c.) learn new skills for
       tomorrow.
21. I am usually striving to
    a. inspire people.
    b. understand underlying
       principles.
    (c.) get better results.

What option do you think John Meyers should pursue? What counsel would you offer him? What would you do if you were John?

CHOOSING OPTIONS

Now that you've had a chance to consider John Meyers' circumstances and dilemma, decide which of the three possible options will best enhance John's career. Read your preferred option first. Then consider the other two.

OPTION A. BUILD ON YOUR POWERWORKING STRENGTH

You decide that your future depends on doing more Power-Work. If you can just work harder, faster and smarter, producing more results with less cost, the company, you assume, will be forced to recognize and reward your contribution.

Immediately, you begin a jogging routine each morning, coming to work an hour earlier than usual and staying an hour later, with a little help from multiple cups of coffee. You cut

Figure 6.2. Dominant work preferences scoring sheet.

Circle the letters you chose. Then total the number of circled letters in each column to determine your dominant work dimension.

Name: John Meyers
Date: December 16, 1995

Question	PowerWork	NetWork	ValueWork
1.	ⓐ	b	c
2.	ⓑ	c	a
3.	ⓒ	a	b
4.	ⓐ	b	c
5.	ⓑ	c	a
6.	c	ⓐ	b
7.	ⓐ	b	c
8.	b	ⓒ	a
9.	c	a	ⓑ
10.	ⓐ	b	c
11.	ⓑ	c	a
12.	ⓒ	a	b
13.	a	ⓑ	c
14.	ⓑ	c	a
15.	c	a	ⓑ
16.	ⓐ	b	c
17.	ⓑ	c	a
18.	c	ⓐ	b
19.	a	ⓑ	c
20.	b	ⓒ	a
21.	ⓒ	a	b
Total	13	6	2
	PowerWork	NetWork	ValueWork

down on breaks, and you eliminate discussions about Hakeem Olajuwon's baseline jumper, working tirelessly to increase your efficiency at running staff meetings by preparing detailed agendas, progress reports, and team performance measures well in advance. You doggedly complete all required management reports on time, double check their accuracy, and amplify the information they contain. With a very defined set of benchmarks, you carefully measure your success and that of your division.

As you feverishly strive to accomplish more each day, you find it increasingly difficult to keep track of all your priorities, and you wish you could add a few hours to your workday. To overcome this new problem, you enroll in a *Daytimer,* time management training course and begin using a day planner system to organize your days. Over the weeks, you maintain a detailed log of your daily activities. When you evaluate the log to see what events and meetings consume most of your time, you discover that many of the meetings do not directly relate to your specific job, so you scale back your meetings schedule even more.

On another track you see that many of your division's critical projects have a lot of interruptions. Thus you decide to redesign much of the division's work flow to link related activities together and eliminate wasted time, energy, and unnecessary work activities. This reengineering does make you and your division even more efficient, and you take no small pride in the fact that you have made clear progress toward your overriding goal of producing more work output by eliminating distractions.

Building upon your PowerWorker strength has energized you and restored much of your flagging enthusiasm and optimism. You are more in control of your career. Your self-confidence rises with all the new-found knowledge of the facts and figures surrounding your division. You maintain the accelerated work schedule and discipline yourself to handle the additional stress and strain on yourself and your family.

Unfortunately, you see less and less of that strain merely because you're not at home to see it. When Deborah suggests a trial separation, saying, "John, we need time apart to figure out where our marriage has gone off track," you suggest that you both enter therapy. When your son's grades drop and your daughter's guidance counselor alerts you to a possible alcohol problem, you blow up and tell them both to "get with the program." Bill buries his head in his arms, and Jennifer storms out of the room, shouting, "Dad, we're not on the company payroll!" With so much chaos and confusion at home, you increasingly seek solace within the comfortable confines of your well-organized office and reorganized work routines.

On the plus side, your efforts at work do not go unnoticed by senior management, who praise your "extra hours of work," and say how much they like the "new John Meyers." They seem genuinely impressed with the level of detail in your reports and compliment you on the "rigorous discipline" you've brought to your division.

As the months roll by, however, you begin to question how much longer you can continue with the program yourself. Your daughter's words haunt you, and you feel a weakening of your energy level. Your health begins to suffer from the early morning, late night, and weekend work, and to make matters worse, all the praise you heard a few months ago from your supervisors seems to have waned. Now you live with a new set of expectations that you will continue to work at this level of intensity indefinitely. "If I back off now," you muse, "I will be in more trouble than before." You're the same old rat running on the same old treadmill, after all, because all of your extra work has thrown your home life into disarray without positioning you any more advantageously within the company. You still manage a chemical additives division, and while your prospects for promotion may have improved slightly, you have now established an almost unbearable routine for yourself that will only expand if and when you win that longed-for promotion.

Option B. Improve Your NetWorking Capability

You decide to improve your NetWorking by first updating and augmenting your technical and managerial skills, then deploying them more broadly throughout the organization. Major changes in the field of chemical engineering require that you refuel your own technical competence, and a host of new management techniques impel you to broaden your understanding of business and organizational leadership.

To accomplish both goals, you enroll in a specialized "engineering update" course offered during the evenings at a nearby university, and you also attend a series of seminars dealing with organizational management in today's work environment.

Furthermore, you scan periodicals in the field of technology management, and regularly participate in a special "forum" on the Internet that includes chemical plant operating simulations. Then you spend time studying the corporate directory so that you can greet your employees by name.

All your efforts to develop your skills and find new ways to apply your expertise prove to be time consuming, quickly pushing you beyond your comfort zone. It humbles you to admit that you've neglected your continuing education in recent years, and you feel awkward trying to sell yourself to others within the company. You have never felt so vulnerable and exposed.

However, as you expand your capabilities, you find a new connection between your love for technology and your desire to make better management decisions. Through the application of a newly developed computer-based operating simulation software program, you learn how to monitor and predict the pattern of critical variables in the operation of your own chemical additives division. Within a few short weeks, your new insights into quality management, operational control, and employee empowerment greatly enhance your capability as a division manager.

To your surprise, your renewed optimism and confidence at work transfer to your home life. Although you have spent a great deal of time away from home in courses and seminars, your growing contentment proves contagious with Deborah and your children, Bill and Jennifer. When you're happier, they're happier. You carve out more quality time with each of them—taking trips to Yellowstone National Park and volunteering time as a baseball coach—because those relationships mean even more to you than the new relationships you are forging in your career.

Forging relationships becomes a dominant goal in your work life as you solicit the support of DuPont's technology division and discuss computer simulations with other division managers and chemical engineers. Before long, you join a companywide project team charged with the development of operating simulation programs for the entire company. Your leadership courses have equipped you to influence the team without dominating or controlling the entire project or becoming frustrated with the time it takes to weigh others' points of view.

As you work with the operating simulation developers, adding your own perspective and opinions, the team gradually solidifies behind a new customized system that goes well beyond what you had originally imagined and fits the needs of DuPont perfectly. The team leader expresses particular appreciation over your awareness of the field, your judgment, and your ability to articulate the benefits of the simulation program. Within a few weeks, you receive requests to explain the system to other managers in other divisions and departments, and before long you are spending a third of your time providing special assistance and instructing others in the use of the simulation technology and software. Senior management takes special note of your contribution. As one senior executive remarks to the team, "John's showing us a whole new way of growing with fresh skills and teamwork."

Although that praise pleases you, it pales by comparison to your family's support. "Dad," says Jennifer, after you and your family win the volleyball tournament at the division's annual picnic, "We're the A-team!"

It doesn't take long for senior management to ask you to spearhead a companywide roll-out of the new operating simulation system. The increased exposure opens up new avenues for your career, and within a year you win a promotion to become Vice President of Information Technology Systems at corporate headquarters.

OPTION C. OVERCOME YOUR WEAKNESS IN VALUEWORKING

You decide to concentrate on ValueWork with a vision for creating greater value for your division's customers. You begin by increasing your contact with external customers and key suppliers, probing them for insights into their needs and concerns. At the same time, you carefully read chemical processing industry research reports and the commentaries of industry futurists.

Over a period of months, you gradually identify a major customer need that neither DuPont nor its competitors have successfully addressed, namely that customers would like a quicker response to small customized orders. To fulfill this desire, you conclude that your division should establish a network of smaller "miniplants" located closer to major customers and offering them greater flexibility.

As you promote this idea by making presentations that detail the extent of the need and explain how your solution can meet it, senior management pays close attention. Before long, you are challenged by some unanticipated questions from those in the company who have spent a lot more time than you have with key customers. Basically, these questions question your assumption that customers really want quicker access to plants and greater customization of their orders. It soon becomes apparent, as you defend your stance, that you have jumped to some premature conclusions about customer needs. While it is true that most customers express needs from time to time that demand timely customization, the majority of such customized chemical additive formulas are not a continuing need and rarely represent the bulk of their orders. In addition, implementing a miniplant strategy would increase the costs of the typical chemical formulations that most customers order. Few customers would sacrifice lower costs on their bulk purchases to gain quicker access to customized formulas that do not represent the majority of their purchases.

Your idea quickly dies and causes you great personal embarrassment. In the end, your premature move raises new doubts in the minds of senior management about whether you "have what it takes to advance further in the company." Fourteen months later, you find yourself included in a new round of downsizing layoffs, bringing your 15-year career with the company to an end.

Although you now find a lot of idle time on your hands to pursue the job hunt, you feel so depressed over losing your job that your presence at home causes more tension than your absence ever did. As your job search continues, you take more and more of your frustrations out on Deborah, Bill, and Jennifer, and they begin to avoid you. Deborah goes to work in a law office as an administrative assistant to help out financially, but you resent the fact that she's become the sole breadwinner. Your loss of self-esteem pushes your children away from you at the very time when they need you the most. How did you let things get so out of control?

ASSESSING YOUR OWN DOMINANT WORK DIMENSION

The John Meyers scenario simplifies reality, but it should have prompted you to think about your own work dimension preferences and how you can best move further toward MetaWorking. To become a MetaWorker, you must do two things: First, identify your own dominant work dimension so that you can temper as well as exploit your natural biases; second, always choose the work dimension that best matches the needs of your particular situation. In the case of John Meyers, Option B proved to be the most productive. In your case, the options will vary, depending on your own unique performance, talents, and goals.

To determine your own dominant work dimension, complete the Dominant Work Preference Indicator (Figure 6.3) now for yourself. With it you can determine whether you should do more PowerWork, develop more NetWork, or discover more ValueWork. Keep in mind that there are no right or wrong answers and that these questions give you only a cursory assessment of your natural work preferences and orientations.

After completing this evaluation, determine your dominant work dimension by filling out the scoring sheet (Figure 6.4) that follows.

As you review your score, keep in mind that although people can and should strive to work in all three dimensions, everyone usually prefers one over the others. If your score on the Dominant Work Preference Indicator splits almost evenly between

Figure 6.3. Dominant work preferences indicator.

Circle the answer that appeals to you most or describes you best.

Name: _____

Date: _____

1. In a group setting, I enjoy
   a. solving immediate problems.
   b. learning about what others think.
   c. discussing new approaches and methods.

2. I get along best with
   a. scientific people.
   b. realistic people.
   c. artistic people.

3. I am viewed by others as
   a. persuasive.
   b. visionary.
   c. practical.

4. I prefer planning that is based on
   a. facts.
   b. values.
   c. logic.

5. I think about business strategy in terms of
   a. a clear vision.
   b. a detailed plan.
   c. an orchestration of talent.

6. In communicating with others in the organization, I am usually
   a. empathetic.
   b. knowledgeable.
   c. factual.

7. In the midst of a chaotic situation, I strive to
   a. get organized.
   b. remain flexible.
   c. search for a new path.

8. I get most excited about
   a. ideas and principles.
   b. things and events.
   c. relationships and people.

9. I take pride in
   a. looking at things differently.
   b. facilitating change.
   c. being realistic.

10. I look on the mistakes of others with
    a. judgment.
    b. understanding.
    c. tolerance.

11. In my personal life, I search for
    a. truth.
    b. good works.
    c. meaning.

12. I take pride in being
    a. a feeling person.
    b. a thinking person.
    c. a doing person.

13. When evaluating business, I like to think in terms of
    a. daily realities.
    b. human potential.
    c. technological possibilities.

14. I prefer change that is
    a. ingenious and sweeping.
    b. incremental and step-by-step.
    c. continuous and challenging.

15. I am most likely to
    a. keep and develop an employee who is delivering unacceptable performance.
    b. terminate an employee for unacceptable performance.
    c. ask for assistance from corporate human resources.

16. After receiving information, I come to conclusions by
    a. evaluating the details.
    b. looking for insights.
    c. identifying the principles involved.

17. In business, I prefer understanding
    a. the economic logic before addressing operating details.
    b. the operating details before worrying about the full picture.
    c. the people issues before dealing with any operating details.

18. I work to enhance organizational capabilities by
    a. introducing new approaches.
    b. conceiving of breakthrough approaches.
    c. improving existing approaches.

19. I attempt to improve results from people by
    a. giving them clear instructions.
    b. applauding their strivings.
    c. pointing out their failings.

(continued)

Figure 6.3. *(Continued)*

20. I believe that the best way to prepare for the future is to
    a. boldly invent tomorrow.
    b. find success today.
    c. learn new skills for tomorrow.

21. I am usually striving to
    a. inspire people.
    b. understand underlying principles.
    c. get better results.

two or all three work dimensions, it could signify one of three things: 1) too much ambivalence or uncertainty in your responses (review your choices); 2) a natural preference for combining two work dimensions (see Figure 6.5); or 3) movement

Figure 6.4. Dominant work preferences scoring sheet.

Circle the letters you chose. Then total the number of circled letters in each column to determine your dominant work dimension.

Question	PowerWork	NetWork	ValueWork
1.	a	b	c
2.	b	c	a
3.	c	a	b
4.	a	b	c
5.	b	c	a
6.	c	a	b
7.	a	b	c
8.	b	c	a
9.	c	a	b
10.	a	b	c
11.	b	c	a
12.	c	a	b
13.	a	b	c
14.	b	c	a
15.	c	a	b
16.	a	b	c
17.	b	c	a
18.	c	a	b
19.	a	b	c
20.	b	c	a
21.	c	a	b
Total	_____	_____	_____
	PowerWork	NetWork	ValueWork

Figure 6.5. The fourth dimension and the natural development track.

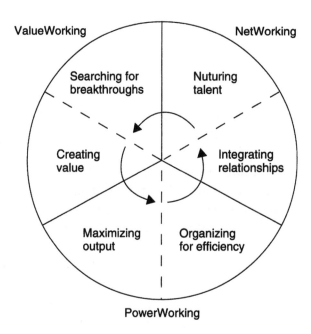

toward MetaWorking. Figure 6.5 shows the two most common work activities in each of the three dimensions as well as what we call the Natural Development Track (the arrows pointing counterclockwise) toward becoming a MetaWorker.

Let's assume you score 10 in NetWorking, 10 in ValueWorking, and 1 in PowerWorking on the Dominant Work Preference Indicator. First, review your responses to the questions, making sure you have selected answers that best describe you when in your most natural and comfortable circumstances. If you feel still comfortable with your split scores you probably, through natural preference or concerted effort, are most comfortable nurturing talent and searching for breakthroughs, a hybrid of NetWorking and ValueWorking. However, if your split score signifies movement toward the balance and wholeness of Meta-Working, you may be a natural NetWorker who has pursued the natural developmental track toward more ValueWorking.

Many people find the Natural Development Track to be a sensible path as they move from a strength in one dimension to greater strength in the other two dimensions, but most people find it difficult to strengthen the last dimension along their development track, as you shall soon see.

UNDERSTANDING AND APPLYING DOMINANT WORK DIMENSIONS

When one work dimension looms as a natural strength, it stands to reason that one of the other two dimensions will represent a primary weakness. The very characteristics that give a person strength in one work dimension are those that work against development in another dimension. Understanding your strength helps you also to understand your weaknesses. The following chart (Table 6.1) illustrates the most common strength and weakness pairings among the three dimensions of work.

Consider your role playing of John Meyers again. As a born PowerWorker, you ran into the most trouble trying to discover ValueWork. By building on your dominant dimension of Power-Working, you achieved a marginal boost to your career as you worked harder, faster, and smarter. But you only worsened your already overstressed life and created a new level of unrealistic expectations that merely reaffirmed to your superiors what they already knew: you are a great PowerWorker. In contrast, you progressed the most when you set out to improve your Net-Working. By pushing the development of your talents and seeking broader relationships for the better deployment of those talents, you made a more significant contribution. Then because of your PowerWorking strength, you outshone those with a natural inclination toward NetWorking but with a weakness in PowerWorking.

In general, we recommend that you follow the path of least resistance as you take your initial steps toward becoming a MetaWorker: while continuing to build on your dominant di-

Table 6.1. Strength–weakness pairings

If Your Strongest Work Dimension Is . . .	Your Weakest Work Dimension Will Be . . .	Reasons Why
PowerWork	ValueWork	• Natural PowerWorkers focus on details and facts rather than on ideas and the big picture, which makes it particularly difficult for them to embrace ValueWork without feeling awkward. • Natural PowerWorkers possess a bias for action and don't always appreciate the need to spend more time discovering breakthroughs.
NetWork	PowerWork	• Because natural NetWorkers often work through others, they do not feel the need to do PowerWork themselves. • Natural NetWorkers sometimes feel they've finished their work once the team has achieved a sense of common purpose and set its goals.
ValueWork	NetWork	• Natural ValueWorkers sometimes find it hard to relate to others. • Natural ValueWorkers regard their discoveries as so self-evident that they spend little time worrying about convincing others of the value of their breakthroughs.

Table 6.2. Strengthening latent work dimensions

If I want to Be Better At . . .	Use PowerWorking to . . .	Use NetWorking to . . .	Use ValueWorking to . . .
PowerWork	• Do the right things and do them the right way to get results. (See Chapter 3.)	• Find and establish partnerships with those whose talents will increase your efficiency and effectiveness.	• Discover breakthroughs in ways to achieve greater cost efficiency and effectiveness.
NetWork	• Work faster and better to eliminate any barriers that prevent development or deployment of talent.	• Develop talents and relationships that build individual and collective competence. (See Chapter 4.)	• Discover new ways to develop capabilities and deploy talent.
ValueWork	• Reengineer the discovery process.	• Link up with those who can assist in the discovery and implementation of new ideas and approaches.	• Discover useful knowledge and apply it to produce breakthroughs. (See Chapter 5.)

mension, focus on improving your next greatest strength. For the PowerWorker, that means concentrating on NetWorking. The NetWorker should concentrate on ValueWorking, and the ValueWorker should focus on PowerWorking. Once you have improved your ability in the work dimension for which you are neither dominant nor weak, you can then turn your attention to your weakest dimension and finally achieve a transformation into the fourth dimension.

STRENGTHENING LATENT WORK DIMENSIONS

As John Meyers, you could not easily accomplish ValueWork by yourself because it represented your weak dimension. Let's take another look at the original scenario. If you, acting as John, had developed NetWorking before the company passed you over for promotion, you would not have tried to perform Value-Work all by yourself. By understanding and applying NetWorking you could have enlisted the help of natural ValueWorkers to discover breakthroughs in your division.

As you work to improve your own capabilities in a latent work dimension, you can use your understanding of the other two dimensions to help you on your way to the fourth dimension. The grid on page 160 (Table 6.2) can guide you toward becoming stronger in each of the three work dimensions by helping you to tap all three as you strive to grow in a single dimension.

You can always enhance your ability to work in one dimension by applying the benefits of all three MetaWorking dimensions to any task. As you can see from the guidelines, MetaWorking can actually help you perform at higher levels in any single dimension or in all three dimensions.

In the next chapter we explore ways in which teams or groups can use the MetaWork system to achieve the next level of performance.

CHAPTER SEVEN

Team
Transformations

"I am a part of all that I have met."

Tennyson

A METAWORK EXERCISE FOR TRANSFORMING TEAM PERFORMANCE

Imagine yourself as a senior marketing executive of Cardon Outdoor Gear, even though doing so makes you feel as if you are on an endangered species list. Cardon's line of sportswear has been languishing for over a year, a turn of events that is especially disappointing given the rapid growth of the 15-location specialty retailer each year since its founding in 1989. In those boom years, customers responded eagerly to Cardon's unique mix of the rugged fabrics and features required for such strenuous outdoor sports activities as mountain climbing and backpacking. Cardon's line of sports goods capitalized beautifully on the consumer trend toward a more physical, rugged look in clothes, even among city folk. But now, only seven years later, consumer tastes have swung to more lightweight gear, and Cardon's management cannot decide how to respond to the situation.

As a first step, Cardon's CEO, Brenda Cardon, organizes a special SWAT team consisting of ten individuals from various disciplines within the company, including marketing, design, store operations, manufacturing, and finance. Considering the nature of the company's predicament, she appoints you to lead the SWAT team, assess the situation, and develop a plan of action. The other nine members of your team possess a broad range of experience and expertise, each one bringing different skills and dominant work dimension preferences to the project: six natural PowerWorkers, two natural NetWorkers, and two natural ValueWorkers. You, as a natural NetWorker, possess strong skills in developing the talents of others and building alliances and relationships. The team easily falls in step behind your leadership.

The night before the first team meeting, you review the agenda while winding down in your jacuzzi. You are concerned about directing your team to a timely but thoughtful solution. Above all else, you want to guide your team's efforts toward results. In your experience with other team projects, the personalities of the members have sometimes clashed irreconcilably or team members have wandered aimlessly for months without ever reaching any conclusions. You are convinced that you must take care to avoid such pitfalls. As a skilled NetWorker, you fundamentally believe in the collective wisdom of the group and realize that a group decision will get better results than the decision of any single individual, but you also recognize the strong personalities of your nine fellow team members.

Your situation represents a common one in business today: A group of people receive an assignment with a clearly defined objective, but with few details showing exactly how to accomplish that objective. With the growth of teams in corporate America, more and more people find themselves thrust into intense short-term team situations requiring that they learn to work with others smoothly and successfully. Some people find it easy; others find it impossible. As team members or leaders, most people will confront such situations again and again in their business careers.

As you get out of the hot tub, you accidentally drop a page of your agenda in the water. You hope it isn't an omen of things to come.

You wrestle with the crucial question: How your team can best approach the problem of reorganizing Cardon's languishing sports clothing line? During the first two SWAT team meetings, members of the group get acquainted and discuss the project's objective, but although you feel good about this early progress, you realize that coming to a group decision will prove even more difficult than you first imagined. You also feel mounting pressure from Brenda Cardon, the company CEO and majority stockholder, who wants a quick resolution to the sports line issue. Now you must determine how your team will reach its conclusion. While this may seem to be a premature concern at such an early stage of deliberation, your strength as a NetWorker and your experience with other teams has taught you that settling on a methodology for reaching a conclusion must occur early in the team-formation stage because that methodology must guide the team's diverse expectations and preferences toward its goal. With this in mind, you boil the viable possibilities down to three:

Option A: Let the majority rule.

Option B: Follow your own instincts.

Option C: Organize around the work.

If you select the first option, you will simply inform the team that after thorough analysis, discussion, and development of solution alternatives, each team member will vote on the best alternative, with the majority ruling the day. Should you choose the second option, you will carefully weigh all analyses, discussions, opinions, and alternatives with people inside and outside the team, and then assume responsibility for recommending the final course of action. The third option differs from the first two because it emphasizes process rather than outcome. If you choose this option, you will not worry about what decision the team should make, but about how the work should be organized to solve the problem. What option will you choose?

MAKING CHOICES

Now that you've weighed the situation, decide which of the three options will deliver the best solution to Cardon's problem. First read your preferred choice; then study the other two.

OPTION A. LET THE MAJORITY RULE

In deciding to allow the team's majority opinion to rule the decision, you encourage an open exchange of information and foster freewheeling discussion of all issues. Given your own NetWorking style, you trust your ability to manage the team and keep the meetings moving toward their ultimate goal. You enjoy helping the team to resolve their differences and find points of agreement, and you firmly believe that through their combined expertise and insight, the team members will, in the end, make the best and most well-informed decision. You build into the process many opportunities for team members to educate one another, discuss their findings, and collaborate on their recommendations. You work especially hard to draw out the opinions and ideas of the less vocal participants. Everyone knows that the final decision will depend on a team vote and that the opinion of the majority will rule.

During the very first team meeting, it becomes quite clear that most people view the high cost of the rugged clothing line as a key issue, and that the solution to the present problem lies in reducing costs. As Diedre O'Connell, the representative from manufacturing, puts it, "Our costs are simply too high compared to our competition. We can't afford to waste time exploring a lot of unrelated issues or analyzing other problems. I have done the research, and I can prove that product cost is the real problem. Let's shift our emphasis right now to considering how to reengineer our processes in order to reduce cost. Don't you all agree?"

Many in the group do agree. When Bill Taylor from finance raises a question about other factors at play, O'Connell and her faction want vehemently to dismiss that action. As team leader, however, you strongly believe that the group should consider other points of view, so you steer the discussion toward a deeper understanding of changing consumer preferences, new dynamics in the marketplace, and competitor responses. Reluctantly, most group members, except for O'Connell, agree that such variables deserve consideration, and the team hammers out a general plan of study. At the next meeting individuals accept specific assignments, agree to reporting deadlines, and express satisfaction that the team has begun making real progress toward its goal. You, too, feel pleased. The initial meetings have gone smoothly and the team knows exactly how to pursue its goal.

Over the next few weeks, the group continues to discuss the issues, thoroughly debating the pros and cons of cutting costs and increasing efficiency. The PowerWorkers, led by Diedre O'Connell, present an impressive report on Cardon's costs, comparisons with competitors, market share projections, and price point information. Bill Taylor from finance, a Value-Worker by nature, finds this report especially enlightening. As the team explores the data, those members most familiar with these facts and figures begin to assert their dominance.

As the PowerWork approach to the situation gains momentum, the team formulates a plan for reengineering Cardon's design-to-production processes, recommending that certain processes change radically to accelerate new designs and that all manufacturing move to outsourced foreign companies that can produce new products more cheaply. As the details of this plan come together, the team grows ever more certain that it has chosen the right course for the company. O'Connell's position wins majority approval, even the vote of once-skeptical Bill Taylor. After reviewing the full plan, at the final team meeting, the team unanimously endorses O'Connell's cost-cutting program and submits it to Brenda Cardon and senior management, who praise the team for its timely and effective work. Impressed with the detailed recommendations, concise action steps, supportive data, and clear sense that the team knows exactly what to do, Brenda Cardon promotes you to the position of Executive Vice President and asks you to oversee the implementation of your recommendations.

Within six months, new lighter-weight apparel reaches the market, costs associated with the sports clothing line drop by 38 percent, and overall sales increase by 18 percent. The product line reaches profitability soon thereafter, winning you and your teammates a generous year-end bonus.

Option B. Follow Your Own Instincts

In deciding to trust your own intuition, you carefully listen to input from all team members, but you present to senior management only those recommendations that your instincts commend as the best for solving the problem. Because Brenda Cardon has entrusted you with the team's final recommendations, you stand to gain or lose the most if the recommendations succeed or fail. As the team leader, you feel that you alone can best maintain a comprehensive perspective of all the issues affecting the final recommendations. After all, your perspective matches that of senior management; otherwise, they would not have supported you as team leader.

You tell yourself, "Of course, every team member will actively participate in the process, share their insights and information, and enter into intense discussion, but I will make it perfectly clear from the outset that we'll make no recommendations until I'm comfortable with them."

From the very first team meeting, it becomes clear the manufacturing representative, Diedre O'Connell and the other PowerWorkers believe that the problem stems from the high cost of the clothing line, and that Cardon should therefore focus on reducing costs. O'Connell and her faction strongly suggest limiting further analysis and taking immediate action. As a natural NetWorker, you quickly draw the other NetWorkers into the initial discussions, soliciting their opinions and drawing out their points of view about such issues as customer's values, changing customer preferences, the effects of general economic conditions on the marketplace, shifting customer demographics, and competitor actions. Bill Taylor from finance, a natural ValueWorker, contributes greatly to the discussion. You stress the importance of fully understanding such issues before the team finalizes its recommendation. You also contact others in the company besides those on the team for fresh insights into these issues. As the team braintorms about knowledgeable personnel to contact for inclusion in the project, a lengthy list soon emerges. You tell the team, "I will assume the responsibility for contacting these people to inform them of our project and solicit their input and assistance." You then ask O'Connell and Taylor to help you obtain input from people on the list before the next meeting.

The next few team meetings center around a "return and report" agenda wherein you orchestrate reports from those on the list, occasionally inviting some of them to make formal presentations to the team. Each report triggers a round of discussion, which, in turn, raises more questions and options that result in yet another list of people to interview. In an effort to tap the right expertise, you and the team reach farther and farther out into the organization.

As team meetings extend over several weeks, a growing unrest and dissatisfaction on the part of many team members, especially Diedre O'Connell and the other PowerWorkers, becomes painfully apparent. O'Connell expresses her impatience openly, saying, "We need to conclude this endless detective work and make our recommendations. This project is taking too much time away from our other work. We already know enough to formulate a plan."

However, you do not yet feel comfortable with any of the suggested recommendations, and you continue to obtain input from all of the "right" people. You simply will not proceed until you've researched every source of pertinent information. However, after continued appeals from members of the team to conclude the investigation, you agree to draft a preliminary set of alternatives to be voted on by selected personnel from outside the team. The alternatives include cost cutting, new product designs, celebrity endorsements, customer focus groups, and a new advertising agency to be chosen by a vote of selected personnel from outside the team. As the draft circulates, you are asked by numerous reviewers to discuss various elements of the alternatives. Finally, you believe you've gotten to the "right people," whose views will help shape the best possible course of action.

Unfortunately, the frustration of O'Connell and her supporters reaches Brenda Cardon, who tells you confidentially, "you must wrap up this project and make a recommendation. If you delay any longer, we won't need a plan. The product line will die." Realizing that you have lost some credibility with the CEO, you quickly move to finalize your team's recommendations.

Within three weeks, you and the team finalize a set of recommendations calling for a complete repositioning of the clothing line with heavy advertising in each of the 15 store markets. After a careful review, Brenda Cardon decides to hire a consulting firm that specializes in retailing to develop the final recommendations. She tells you, "Your recommendations may have worked, but they seemed so complicated and required so much additional analysis, spending, and time that we decided to bring in some outside experts to simplify things." Within three months, she promotes Diedre O'Connell to the position of Executive Vice President and asks for your resignation.

OPTION C. ORGANIZE AROUND THE WORK

In deciding to focus your team's efforts on the dimensions of work that surround any business problem, you make sure before the very first team meeting that Brenda Cardon will afford all the time and resources that it will take to solve this particular problem. Lack of resources or an unrealistic timetable will ruin any chance of success. "I assure you," Cardon promises, "I want the right solution, not a quick fix. We'll give you whatever it takes to do this job right." Reassured, you schedule a team meeting later in the day.

During your team's first get-acquainted meeting, you observe each of the nine participants closely. Then at the end you ask each to fill out a Dominant Work Dimension Assessment so that you can get a better feel for each individual's preference for PowerWorking, NetWorking, or ValueWorking. You think this approach may help you tap strengths, strengthen weaknesses, and harmonize the efforts of the whole team in a way that will pull the group into the fourth dimension of MetaWorking.

After taking the assessment yourself, you appreciate your own strength as a NetWorker. After all, that's why Brenda Cardon appointed you to be team leader. The assessments of the nine other team members reveal six PowerWorkers, most notably the representative from manufacturing, Diedre O'Connell; one other NetWorker; and two ValueWorkers. Bill Taylor from finance stands out in the last category. This mix of talent concerns you. You know that this project will require all three dimensions of work, but can you enable the whole group to transcend to the fourth dimension, where you believe the solution to Cardon's problem lies? NetWorkers guide the identification, development, or recruitment of the key talents and relationships required to solve the problem. As a natural NetWorker yourself, you identify others in the company besides your nine teammates who excel in the various dimensions, and you ask senior management to add four more people to your team. Senior management agrees, and you invite two more NetWorkers and two more ValueWorkers to join the group. The new 14-member team now includes six PowerWorkers, four of whom exhibit the ability to work in other dimensions; four Networkers; and four ValueWorkers. This balance pleases you.

During the second team meeting, you help all 14 members to more fully grasp their naturally dominant work dimensions and their primary weaknesses. With this increased awareness, each team member begins to feel confident that he or she can contribute to the team effort, and all realize the need to shore up weaknesses while maintaining strengths at the same time.

As Diedre O'Connell says by the end of this meeting, "Our collective decision will prove best because we can, as a group, move into the fourth dimension."

At the third meeting, team members strive to implement the principles of MetaWorking. They resist the natural inclination to work only in their dominant dimensions. Each seeks out alliances and relationships with those whose dominant work dimensions complement their own, and everybody aims to improve the MetaWorking ability of others. This attitude breaks down the traditional barriers that beset many teams, and your team members succeed in "speaking openly," "removing personal feelings," and "maintaining a focus on the common goal."

A mere three days after assuming responsibility for the team, you are confident about its makeup and commitment. Knowing that group leadership should vary from time to time depending on the issues at hand, you resolve to let the most relevant expertise dominate the group whenever necessary. For instance, when the issues of efficiency and cost cutting arise during the fourth meeting, you allow Diedre O'Connell to take the lead because these issues lend themselves to her superb PowerWorking. When, during the fifth meeting, the issues change to building capabilities and creating customer value, you and Bill Taylor, in turn, assume more leadership.

This fifth meeting marks a significant turning point for the team. All the major issues have come to the table, each promoted by a different individual. Diedre O'Connell has clarified the PowerWorking dimension of the problem, succinctly concluding that "We must include in your recommendation ways to increase efficiency and reduce costs for the sports line." In stating the NetWorking dimension you have said, "Our recommendations must take into account Cardon's existing and needed capabilities in the marketplace, and they must include ways to build key partnerships inside and outside the company that will enable us to develop the needed capabilities." Finally, Bill Taylor has summed up the ValueWorking dimension by insisting, "We must discover more about our customers and what they really value in sports apparel." You are confident that the team has obtained the broadest possible vision of Cardon's problem and clearly sees what the company must do, develop, and discover to solve it.

At this point you suggest that O'Connell, Taylor, and you serve as stewards over each of the three work dimensions to make sure that the project blends and proportions all three dimensions throughout the next stages of the project.

Now the team rolls up its sleeves and sets to work on solving the problem. You remind everyone that this project enjoys Brenda Cardon's full support: "She has given us adequate time to do our work, and although she wants us to move quickly, she assures me that she will invest whatever resources it takes to do it right." With this mandate in mind, the team agrees that they should first focus on ValueWork, spending about 50 percent of their time and resources working in this dimension. Doing so will allow the group to discover the reality of the changing consumer buying patterns and show them how Cardon can create value for its customers. The team also agrees that the work must shift next to NetWorking and PowerWorking, with nearly 20 percent of their time and resources used to marshal necessary talent and develop appropriate relationships, and with the other 30 percent spent in making sure that everything gets implemented with maximum efficiency. Because so many of the issues deal with the final cost of the product to the consumer, the team decides to devote a relatively large portion of the time to PowerWorking.

Within a few short days, the team recommends an immediate upscaling of the sports line to a higher level of quality than that of Eddie Bauer and L.L. Bean. ValueWorkers on the team have discovered that 20 to 25 percent of Cardon's customers would gladly pay premiums to get higher quality sports clothing. Given the groundwork you laid with Brenda Cardon at the outset, the team gains quick approval for implementing this recommendation. Building on the team's initial NetWorking efforts, the company develops necessary supplier and outsourcing relationships and partnerships almost overnight. L.L. Bean's head sportswear designer comes aboard, and Cardon initiates the takeover of a struggling eight-store sporting goods chain. Then, within 30 days after receiving approval to implement its recommendation, the team moves into a concerted PowerWorking program that touches every nook and cranny of the organization with the goal of controlling costs while upscaling the sports clothing line. Then 90 days later, Cardon introduces its new line of sportswear in time for the Christmas shopping season. By year-end, sales of the line increase by 54 percent, with profits rising 112 percent. Brenda Cardon promotes you to the newly created position of Vice President of Strategic Planning, and all 14 members of the team receive generous year-end bonuses.

METAWORK'S TEAM PHILOSOPHY

The Cardon example should ring true for anyone who has ever led or participated in a project team intent on accomplishing an objective. With the advent of more teamwork in business, much advice has appeared on how to make teams more effective by mastering the dynamics of the people involved, but we think the MetaWork system provides the simplest and most powerful means for doing so because it exploits, rather than compromises, the differences among team members. MetaWorkers come to a project team not only with a clear understanding of individual differences, but also with an undying commitment to harness those differences for superachievement. Although MetaWorkers seek proficiency in all three work dimensions, they readily recognize their own natural strengths and weaknesses. This understanding, coupled with the belief that each person can create value, breeds an unusually strong sense of confidence, appreciation, and collaboration among all team members.

Team MetaWorkers also enjoy a heightened understanding of the true value of teamwork. Whether formally or informally organized into groups, MetaWorkers constantly form "teams" to accomplish the highest goals, reaching out to those whose work abilities complement their own. By gaining a heightened awareness of others' strengths, and by blending these diverse strengths toward a desired objective, MetaWorkers and their teammates enter the fourth dimension.

As the third option in the Cardon example depicts, the MetaWorking team (MetaTeam) rarely gets hung up on the issue of who should lead the team. They know that the work, rather than the person, must dictate the agenda, and that leadership will shift to those who can make the greatest contributions at any given point in time. This basic concept, that the work itself forms the focal point around which MetaTeams organize themselves, represents the essence of the MetaWorking team philosophy. Rather than focusing on the personalities of the team, MetaTeams always focus on ways to improve the work for accomplishing the task at hand because they know that MetaWorking represents not only a means to an end, but an end in itself.

APPLYING THE METAWORK PROJECT PLANNING TOOL

As you have seen, Team MetaWorking involves collectively increasing the ability of each member and the entire team to work in the fourth dimension, organizing the team, and deploying its talents in ways that appropriately blend, proportion, and sequence PowerWorking, NetWorking, and ValueWorking. The MetaWorking Project Planning Tool (Figure 7.1) can help you pursue this ultimate dimension of teamwork.

Team members and leaders can employ the MetaWork Project Planning Tool to prepare for a project, to orient team members toward the right work, to track each work dimension, and to promote a project's overall progress. The tool consists of seven key sections:

1. Description of the project

2. Conditions affecting the project

3. Work needed in each dimension

4. Work dimension sequence

Figure 7.1. MetaWork project planning tool.

Project Title	Project Leader	Project Assigned by	Date Assigned	Date Due

Project Team   *PowerWorkers*   *NetWorkers*   *ValueWorkers*

Objectives of the Project

Conditions Affecting the Project

Time   *Resources*   *Significance to Company*

Work Sequence   Work Proportion   Steward   Key Dates

1. What needs to be Discovered? ValueWork
"Greatest Value for Greatest Numbers"

2. What needs to be Developed? NetWork
"Greatest Capabilities for Greatest Advantage"

Work Sequence	Steward
Work Proportion	Key Dates

3. What needs to be Done? PowerWork
"Greatest Results for Least Costs"

Work Sequence	Steward
Work Proportion	Key Dates

5. Work dimension proportions

6. Work dimension stewards

7. Milestone and completion dates

Let's take a closer look at each of these seven sections.

DESCRIPTION OF THE PROJECT

This description section of the tool records general information about the project title, team leader, assigned team members, due date, and project objective. It also notes the dominant work dimensions of the assigned team members allowing the team leader to review or reconfigure the makeup of the team before proceeding. If a team member's dominant work preference is not known, that teammate should take the Dominant Work Preference Assessment presented in Chapter Six.

As we have learned from our own experience, the expert opinions of practicing psychiatrists and psychologists coupled with psychological research from data bases, such as the *Myers-Briggs Type Indicator,* all suggest that there is a natural predominance of PowerWorkers in the overall work force. In the general working population, approximately 65 percent of all people will identify PowerWorking as their dominant dimension, with approximately 35 percent splitting their identifications between NetWorking and ValueWorking. Many natural PowerWorkers find themselves attracted to the field of management and business because most companies place a high value on the ability to "get things done efficiently and effectively." Natural Net-Workers often feel drawn to communication-intensive work such as advertising and public relations, journalism and publishing, arts and entertainment, and politics. Natural ValueWorkers often go into knowledge-intensive fields such as technological research and development, higher education in scientific and technical areas, product design, and software engineering. Regardless of the mix represented by a given team, the best results tend to come from the right balance and integration of talents.

This description section also stresses the objectives of the project and the conditions surrounding it. Had the Cardon team not pinpointed its objective and determined senior management's level of commitment (time and resources) to achieving that objective, the project would have been doomed from the start.

CONDITIONS AFFECTING THE PROJECT

Every team operates under certain conditions that will affect the outcome of the project. These conditions may include organizational constraints or parameters within which the team must operate, the availability of resources, time requirements, or a host of other possibilities. For example, in the most positive Cardon scenario, the team leader was confident about the schedule as well as the availability of resources because the CEO had given assurances concerning both. In some cases, the resource constraints may affect not only the composition of the project team and its level of support, but also what the team can recommend as a viable course of action.

The significance of the project to the overall well-being of the company should always receive a lot of attention up front. Does the project address a chronic problem within the company that could, unless fixed, jeopardize the company's future? What will happen to the organization if this project fails? What will happen if it succeeds? Answers to such questions can profoundly affect the timing, sequencing, or proportioning of the work dimensions.

Extended conditions may also affect both the team's effort and its final recommendations. Changing market conditions, new competitor strategies, technological advancements, and fluctuating customer needs may all conspire to force the team in one direction or another.

Work Needed in Each Dimension

Discussions about the work needed in each dimension should include the entire team. Individual input and the collective insight gained from the group can best determine what the team must accomplish in each dimension.

Quite often a team begins with ValueWork by asking, "What must we discover?" (This is the first question of the MetaWork Project Planning Tool.) For each team project, regardless of its nature or its specific goals, new discoveries can create new value for customers. By asking this basic question, the team focuses first and foremost on creating that value. Follow-up questions can further enhance the discussion of ValueWorking, resulting in a list of needed discoveries:

- Which customers?

- What do customers currently value?

- How can we add value?

- How can we increase the number of customers?

At this stage of its work, the team does not actually make the discoveries, but determines areas that the team should explore.

The second basic question, "What must we develop?" focuses attention on the capabilities, competencies, and relationships required for success. Follow-up questions include these:

- What core competencies do we need to develop or acquire before we can deliver value to our customers?

- Do we possess those competencies and talents now?

- Can we acquire those competencies?

- How can we nurture and integrate the talents we currently possess?

- What key relationships and partnerships inside and outside the company should we form to increase our capabilities?

These questions can help the team assess competitive positioning and break down the organizational barriers preventing a more useful deployment of resources and talent.

The third question, "What must we do?", turns attention toward efficiency and effectiveness in producing results and reducing costs. Supplemental questions might include the following:

- How can we better organize operations to increase efficiency?

- How can we maximize resources?

- Can we reengineer work processes to improve efficiency and effectiveness?

The practical discussion flowing from such questions can lead to significant improvements in a variety of operations, systems, processes, and procedures.

WORK DIMENSION SEQUENCE

This section from the MetaWork Project Planning Tool identifies the best sequence for performing work in each of the three work dimensions. Because project conditions often affect the work sequence, sequencing scenarios should honor the most common project conditions (see Table 7.1).

WORK DIMENSION PROPORTIONS

During the initial stages of a project, the team should try to determine the proportional emphasis that each dimension will receive. Working in the fourth dimension requires constant and careful judgment about which dimension to emphasize or stress at each stage as the project unfolds. Basing their judgment on

Table 7.1. Project conditions and work sequences

If Project Conditions are . . .	Work Sequence should be . . .
Limited **time** to complete the project; then . . .	PowerWork should take center stage because it will produce the quickest results.
Limited **resources** available for this project; then . . .	NetWork should occur first because it can develop talents and capabilities more cost effectively through alliances and partnerships.
Tremendous **significance** of the project to the overall well-being of the company; then . . .	ValueWork should dominate because it creates greater value for more customers.

the same factors that influence the conditions affecting the project and the work sequence, the team should also consider the size of the task and the overall timetable. For example, if team members believe that ValueWork should occur first, but lack sufficient experience in this dimension, they may decide to give it a large portion of their time and effort because it will not occur quickly or easily. However, deciding to spend more time in the ValueWork dimension does not exclude nonnatural ValueWorkers from the process until the need for their dominant dimension rolls around. Rather, it means that all team members will focus on ValueWork as the first and most dominant dimension for the project. Those with a natural inclination toward PowerWorking will ensure that the resulting discoveries are turned into practical and "real" recommendations. Natural NetWorkers will build bridges between the ValueWorkers and the PowerWorkers and continually draw out the expertise of ValueWorkers from both inside and outside the team.

WORK DIMENSION STEWARDS

To ensure that the team moves into the fourth dimension, stewards with preferences in each dimension should accept responsibility for guiding others through their respective realms. The team's best PowerWorker, NetWorker, and ValueWorker should become stewards, respectively, of those dimensions. Each steward will then focus on monitoring the team's effort and success in a specific work dimension so that it is constantly improved. For example, the ValueWork steward will continually push the team to consider value-related issues and will not rest until the team adequately addresses all aspects of this dimension. Stewards, acting as coaches for the team, can raise the overall capacity for Team MetaWorking.

MILESTONE AND COMPLETION DATES

If a team does not accomplish its objective by a target date, it has failed in its mission. This section of the tool helps the team to monitor timely progress toward the final objective. It also identifies key dates for the completion of each dimension of the work. Agreement on milestones and completion dates for each dimension of work will greatly enhance the completion of the entire project on time and within the budget. The team can use the MetaWork Project Planning Tool to help anticipate the entering and exiting of each work dimension required by each stage of the project so that the overall work moves steadily toward the fourth dimension. Continuing in one work dimension, as Cardon's team did in Option B, without perceiving the need for a timely exit, can compromise the success of any project.

CHAPTER EIGHT

Organizational Transformations

"I find the great thing in this world is not so much where we stand, as in what direction we are moving."

Mark Twain

A METAWORK EXERCISE FOR TRANSFORMING ORGANIZATIONAL PERFORMANCE

Imagine yourself as CEO of Digital Robotics, a futuristic organization that you must guide into the twenty-first century.

In the late 1980s, Digital Robotics pioneered a revolutionary manufacturing system centered around a catlike combination of steel, cable, and artificial intelligence. By combining flexible robots and sophisticated software, this company first introduced a machine, Cybermaker, that fully replicated the work of a welder in an automotive assembly plant. Because adjustments in the software could instantly convert Cybermaker's work from passenger cars to heavy duty trucks, and even military hardware applications, the machines quickly attracted customers in every major industry that relied on machine tool manufacturing. Prices of the machine dropped, applications expanded to the plastics and electronics industries, and by the mid-1990s, Digital Robotics' customers included such renowned corporations as Apple Computer, Rubbermaid, SONY, Unibase, and Volkswagen. Digital Robotics helped create the first wave of flexible manufacturing systems, and it continued to ride the crest of that wave for more than ten years, propelling it to the forefront of a brand new industry. Now, you must decide how to invent the company's future.

Welcome to your new job as CEO of an innovative organization on the cutting-edge of American industry. You stroll across the campuslike park that houses corporate headquarters, slide your identification card into the front door of the gleaming chrome and glass administration building, and ride the escalator to your new second-story office suite. You notice the small silver nameplate on your door—Chief Executive Officer—as you step into a room that seems more like the deck of the *Starship Enterprise* than the workspace for a captain of commerce.

This achievement marks a memorable milestone in your rather remarkable career. Now in your midforties, you have enjoyed a wide range of management and senior leadership experiences, including your term as CEO for Flexsoft, one of Digital's key software suppliers. You have shaped your management style to reflect your confidence in others, your enthusiasm and optimism for the future, and your sincere concern for the career development of those with whom you work. More than anything else, this "attitude of caring" attracted Digital Robotics' Board of Directors, convincing them that you could provide long-lasting direction for the company.

You remember the crucial interview with James Fairmont, founder and current Chairman of the Board, who questioned you at length about your ability to work with a wide range of people from DR's elite corps of scientists and inventors to its dedicated cadre of machine-tool specialists and marketing experts. "I've learned one thing over the years," you told him. "The best organizations get results by deploying three kinds of talent. You need people who create value, you need people who can turn that value into products, and you need people who can deliver that value to customers at the right cost. Without all three, not even DR can succeed." Fairmont liked that answer enough to urge the Board to grant you the job of inventing the company's future.

Here you sit, contemplating your first actions as CEO. You power up your PC workstation and call up the menu. Aha! A flashing red arrow appears beside the file labeled, "Fairmont's Log," so you call up that file, which opens with a note from the Chairman: "Welcome aboard! I thought you might want to review a summary of our situation before you set to work."

Fairmont's summary proves to be revealing. During the past several years, the company has racked up impressive growth rates of 25 to 30 percent per year, but that upward curve leveled off dramatically last year. Despite that leveling off, however, R&D continued to expand, pushing many R&D projects over its budget share as a percentage of sales. To make matters worse, customers have begun complaining about the failure rate of their robotics systems. A few years ago, customers had been willing to accept occasional systems failures because the robotics movement was still in its infancy. Now, some seven years later, they will not tolerate such glitches. To address that problem, DR has devoted much of its R&D investment toward finding ways to make systems more secure and to eliminate the down-time that has plagued too many robotics units.

Fairmont's view coincides with your own research into the industry before you accepted the position, and although you could draw few hard and fast conclusions, you sensed that the market was changing rapidly. Your intuition tells you that the fervor for robotics products and systems has waned, and although Fairmont and the Board never raised this growing skepticism during your talks with them, you suspect that, to some degree, it has contributed to DR's current predicament. However, you would have accepted the job anyway because you feel supremely confident in your ability to chart a path through the problem.

Fairmont's summary concludes with a gentle reminder: "I know you can clarify our strategic direction and build a company that will thrive well into the next century. Good luck!"

After you log off from the network, you boil down your mandate to two simple sentences: "This is not a crisis. I must invent an entirely new future for the company, but Fairmont and the Board have given me the time and resources I need to do it right."

With this context firmly in mind, you begin to explore your options. Suppose you applied the MetaWork system to the problem. As you told Fairmont, you appreciate contributions from a wide range of talents, which you might easily label PowerWork, NetWork, and ValueWork. Some workers create value, some put that value into products, and some deliver that value to customers. The Digital Robotics' work force includes all three, although the history of the company reflects a shifting emphasis as it moved from a period of invention to one of applied R&D, and finally, to one of marketing and sales. What emphasis or mix should you pursue now? Clearly, the answer to that question will shape DR's strategic thrust.

To guide your ultimate decision, you conduct a thorough analysis of the company's current status with respect to the three dimensions of work, administering company-wide assessments similar to those in Chapters Three, Four, and Five designed to measure key indicators of PowerWork, NetWork, and Value-Work. The results will, it is hoped, enable you to place your finger on the heartbeat of Digital Robotics' work force.

When the assessment concludes several weeks later, you learn that people in the company emphasize PowerWorking first and foremost, with ValueWorking second, and NetWorking a distant third. Not surprising for a company such as DR, the data also reveal that most of the ValueWorking occurs in the R&D department. Few people outside R&D display Value-Working characteristics, and most managers score high as PowerWorkers. Virtually no one prizes NetWorking. You speculate that the highly competitive marketplace and the company's strong technical orientation has provided fertile ground for an insulated culture in which self-possessed engineers believe they can learn little from others. Your own interaction with key engineers confirms that they generally believe that their discoveries drive the company's success and that they expect other departments, especially manufacturing and marketing, to implement their discoveries and deliver them to customers with the utmost efficiency. This has naturally led to an emphasis on PowerWork in every area outside R&D, especially among senior management.

When you compare DR's assessment with profiles of competitors, you find that a growing number of them have begun stressing strategic alliances as a way to acquire advancing technological knowledge more quickly. In light of this trend toward NetWorking, DR seems out-of-step with its rivals.

Over the next several weeks, you continue meeting with your key managers, attending trade shows, talking with customers, and reviewing the competition. As the web of facts, figures, assessments, and personal perceptions gives you a clearer picture of DR's situation, you realize that you must soon make a decision. Again, sitting alone at your desk, you ponder ways to invent your company's future. Should you continue emphasizing PowerWork, thereby further lowering the cost of robotics equipment and systems? Should you stress NetWork to develop key relationships and partnerships, allowing you to gain access to new technologies that could augment DR's own capabilities? Would it be better, though, to focus on ValueWork and the discoveries that will reinvent the industry? Each option, will, of course, create a distinctly different company with markedly different cultures and competencies.

What option will you choose?

Option A: Continue to emphasize PowerWork.

Option B: Stress NetWork.

Option C: Lead with ValueWork to reinvent the industry.

Before you read about the way your choice will unfold, keep in mind that most senior executives and businesspeople the world over face this sort of dilemma every day. With markets, customer demand, and competitor strategies changing at lightening speed, more and more executives, managers, and employees must struggle to anticipate how the marketplace will change, how competition will react, and where new technology will emerge. The antidote for such uncertainty lies in making choices that combine all three dimensions of work while emphasizing the one that should guide the company's decision making at a given stage of development. Read your choice first, then review the other two.

MAKING CHOICES

Late on a Friday night, over a bowl of "Rocky Road" ice cream, three months after you took the reins as CEO of Digital Robotics, you finally choose a direction for the company's future. By Monday afternoon, that direction takes shape.

OPTION A. CONTINUE TO EMPHASIZE POWERWORK

Chairman Fairmont opens the door of the board room and escorts you to the head of the conference table. The board has requested that you share with them your strategy for the future, scheduling a two-hour meeting during which you will lay out for them the details of your plan.

You preface the discussion with a short speech. "I have decided where I think Digital Robotics should go, and I know exactly how we can get there." The room grows quiet; all eyes stare at you. You proceed confidently: "After a thorough assessment of the market and our customer base, I am convinced that we should stay in the robotics business. Although some of the luster that once surrounded the idea of robotics has lessened, I still foresee a strong market for our systems in the coming years. However, customers are complaining about the high cost of our products, especially in light of their relatively high failure rate. Some customers have realized only marginal increases in productivity, and many prospective customers are reluctant to invest in such expensive technology."

During your speech, you feel a little like Ross Perot as you project a series of graphs on the wall depicting the relationship between the cost of robotics and the benefit they deliver to the customers. You continue: "I am proposing two prongs to our strategy. First, we must drastically lower the cost of our product line to a point where the benefit to the customer increases dramatically. Second, we must hold our technology stable at its current level, greatly reducing our investment in further technological advances for now. In the future, we'll return to aggressive R&D investment, but right now we must focus on cutting the cost of existing technology."

A lively discussion ensues, spearheaded by James Fairmont, who sees this gambit as a dangerous departure from the strategy upon which he founded and built the company. However, you ably deal with all skepticism and convincingly promote your point of view. Three hours later, the Board approves your plan and encourages you to proceed with the utmost speed.

Immediately you set about revitalizing the company's emphasis on PowerWork. All ValueWork shifts away from research that advances the state of the technology and toward finding ways to reduce production costs. R&D engineers quickly begin analyzing ways to redesign and produce complicated robotics machines in less time. With the attention of R&D diverted from new discoveries, you try to close the gap by establishing relationships with key suppliers whose advanced technology will enable DR to gain new machinery and equipment. With such NetWorking, you believe DR can eliminate some capital investment by relying on the discovery capabilities of others instead of internal capabilities.

The main thrust of DR will, however, revolve around Power-Work with its chief focus on reengineering the entire design and production process. To further this cause, you organize a team to study customers' needs and determine how to translate these needs into design requirements, how to turn designs into working prototypes, and how to convert design specifications into production specs and final production. Everyone is geared to the main objective: Eliminate any costly unnecessary steps that delay final production.

You also install a strict set of financial controls, each designed to monitor and improve the management of all the company's resources. Engineers who once enjoyed great flexibility in purchasing the latest technical equipment whenever they wished must now justify every expenditure request. Each department now follows more detailed budgets than ever before, which you monitor on a daily basis. All of this increased financial data enables you to analyze the costs of every contract with every customer and accurately determine the profitability of every single one.

Eight months into the PowerWork program, Digital Robotics enjoys a small increase in profitability, despite a general downturn in the marketplace. The company's emphasis on cost control and on accelerating the time it takes to deliver a customer's order has kept it profitable at a time when many competitors are bleeding red ink. The company's research engineers develop a new software program that can simulate design features on a computer screen and allow customers to "see" how their final robotics systems will look. Customers can add or remove features at will until they are comfortable with the final product. Once the customer is satisfied, DR designs and delivers the unique robotics system with only a few modifications. This reengineered process virtually eliminates the prototyping stage that formerly took two to three months. The big savings in production costs make it possible for Digital to deliver lower-cost systems than any competitor can offer.

The whole culture of DR evolves as well. The maverick engineers and technologists who once strove to expand the "envelope" of their thinking have either changed their approach or left the company. In their place has emerged a breed of engineers whose skills revolve around efficiency, analysis, measurement, benchmarking, and reengineering. Although the culture does not vibrate with freewheeling inventiveness, as it once did, it does display a higher sense of confidence in knowing the details of the business and delivering results with extreme efficiency. The new generation of employees provides you and your executive team with up-to-the-minute information on the status of each contract, the profit or loss for each delivered system, evaluations of each design and production team, and daily reviews of the company's financial position. Employees have accepted the tighter controls of the company as a small price to pay for improved profit sharing and the exhilaration of winning in a tight marketplace. To show their understanding of your closer regulation, they give you a strait jacket filled with Monopoly money for your 44th birthday.

Chairman James Fairmont and the Board of Directors are satisfied with your performance and extend your contract for three years, with 12 percent annual raises and enhanced profit sharing. Two years later, however, the board agrees to a merger with Cybernant, a German conglomerate that has stolen the lead in the emerging field of information systems manufacturing, of which robotics now forms but a small part. Although you win a position in the conglomerate as the Vice President of Manufacturing, you no longer drive the company's strategy, and although you are somewhat deflated by this turn of events, you also feel that you've landed in the right job.

OPTION B. STRESS NETWORK

James Fairmont ushers you into the board room, where you will outline your strategy for the future in a two-hour meeting. You relish this opportunity to share with the board both your vision and your specific plans for implementing it.

You begin confidently by saying, "I am pleased to report that I have decided where I think Digital Robotics should go and how we can get there." The room grows quiet as all eyes turn to you. "I foresee dramatic changes in the market. Customers who once felt excited by the promise of robotics in terms of increased productivity now want more. They have begun looking for additional ways to increase their manufacturing efficiency and gain a stronger edge for their products. They not only desire the benefits of robotics, but they want to link it with management information systems and quality management programs that provide improved controls over production costs. They need more than machines. They need consulting expertise in manufacturing processes and advice on which of the current manufacturing design philosophies will deliver the best results. We have been supplying the machines but have been of little help with the information systems context and the people side of total quality management. Most customers would prefer one source for all of their needs, a source that provides a holistic approach that makes sense. Although DR doesn't currently possess capabilities to make that happen, we can acquire that expertise. Instead of investing our resources to develop these capabilities in house, I propose that we forge a series of strategic partnerships with firms that have already developed them. If we make the right alliances, we could create an unbeatable combination in the marketplace."

This view obviously surprises James Fairmont, who founded and built the company on technical discoveries. He has always resisted alliances of any sort. Although he and some of the older board members question your ideas, the younger members support your plan enthusiastically. Eventually, all agree with your plans and urge you to proceed with this new direction.

Over the next few months, you gingerly test the water, probing here and there for potential relationships among firms that would best serve as partners. Surprisingly, most of them love the idea, making your choice more difficult than you had imagined. The most promising prospect, Andersen Consulting, designs and installs complex information systems for manufacturing enterprises and employs dozens of consultants recognized for their expertise in the field. Andersen immediately sees the potential of a joint venture that would propel it into new markets. After much discussion, you and Andersen hammer out a deal and the partnership begins.

After one year, the alliance with Andersen results in a doubling of Digital Robotics' annual revenue. Within days, the *Wall Street Journal* announces a host of Andersen clients requesting robotics design assistance and advice. Andersen consultants immediately begin including Digital engineers and teams on dozens of projects. Although DR's profits have grown much less than its revenues, due in part to the added expenses of the alliance and the fact that the two companies must now share the benefits, the future opportunities seem unlimited.

Digital's business has changed a lot. Whereas it once operated primarily as a high-tech production house, it now functions as a highly charged intellectual team of experts whose advice and consultation attracts many eager clients. Many reticent DR engineers, who once preferred pure technical research, now enjoy sharing the spotlight with major clients. However, some, unable to deal with this new role, leave the company. The mix of PowerWorking, ValueWorking, and NetWorking varies greatly, depending on the specific consulting team and project. The purchase of robotics at first remained relatively flat, with sales of actual units dropping off slightly, but increased consulting revenues have more than offset the loss.

The prized skills of the DR culture have become project management, teamwork, and considerations of the full context in which the company's systems operate. PowerWorkers focus on improving the efficiency of DR's relationships with clients by reducing the amount of time wasted in unnecessary or improper consulting procedures. The emphasis of the NetWorkers is on building relationships, participating with Andersen consultants on projects, and remaining flexible and adaptive to new settings, circumstances, and client needs. Employees who desired a more tightly controlled environment in which relationships change little have left the company and have been replaced by NetWorkers. DR's management has shifted from working around products to working around client relationships and client projects. You are pleased with the potential of the alliance and see it continuing in new areas originally unforeseen by yourself and Andersen Consulting.

Chairman James Fairmont and the Board of Directors give you high marks for what you've accomplished, extending your contract for three more years, awarding you a $250,000 bonus, and enhancing your profit-sharing plan. Two years later, you accept a position at Andersen Consulting as CEO, a move that ideally suits your NetWorking skills. James Fairmont sells the company he founded to a German conglomerate, Cybernant, that has pioneered the emerging manufacturing information systems field, and starts a new communications systems company with the proceeds. Under your guidance, Andersen forms alliances with both firms that prove beneficial to all concerned.

OPTION C. LEAD WITH VALUEWORK TO REINVENT THE INDUSTRY

Chairman James Fairmont welcomes you to the board room, where you take a seat at the head of the long, chrome and glass conference table. The board has requested that you share with them your strategy for the future in a two-hour meeting during which you intend to lay out for them the details of your vision and the specific steps you will take to implement it. You take a big gulp of ice water.

"I believe that a company must lead, follow, or get out of the way," you tell the board. "Digital Robotics is not a follower, and we're never going to get out of the way. That leaves one option." The room grows quiet as all eyes focus on you. You speak slowly and confidently: "We know that our manufacturing customers are losing their enthusiasm for robotics because the systems simply have not delivered on their promises. Claims of unprecedented increases in productivity have proven overly optimistic. DR has led the way with the best products, of course, but even we can't promote zero system failures and machines that can instantaneously convert to nonstandard shapes. Therefore, I believe our emphasis should shift toward human factors in the workplace." When Chairman Fairmont, who founded and built the company on his vision of the fully automated workplace, questions that assumption, you respond by saying, "Automation will continue, but I foresee information and software becoming more central to the manufacturing process than hardware and machine tools. Information can link the customer closer to the production floor, and software will provide the necessary flexibility to make products tailored to customers' needs. If I am right, Digital can capture that market. We have already created the most effective and most advanced information system to tell our machines what to do. With some modifications, we can deliver what the market now wants—the agility and flexibility for systems to produce the product variations demanded by customers."

You support your point with an impressive array of charts, graphs, and quotes from key Digital customers. The board enters into a lengthy and heated discussion, challenging you every step of the way. You counter each assault with logic and precision, backing your point of view with examples from a dozen different industries. Fairmont sums up the opposition when he says, "Such a thrust represents an entirely new shift for our company, one that will essentially terminate DR as it now stands and turn it into something entirely different." You agree. The future, you argue, will look significantly different, and DR must invest itself to match that future. "DR must," you insist, "remain a leader." After careful consideration, the Board finally agrees to proceed with your vision.

You quickly focus the company's research talent on software and information, organizing an entirely new unit consisting of engineers, production specialists, and software programmers charged with considering how information can better guide production processes. For years, Digital has used software to control the functions of robots, but now you want the company to view that same software structure as the master command code for the entire production process, linking customers to the manufacturing floor for an unprecedented level of responsiveness, customization, and online product experimentation.

Throughout the next year, you dedicate all of the company's efforts to this project. DR continues to fill existing contracts for robotics; it enters into no new ones. All the PowerWorking of DR focuses on facilitating the research and discovery process, finding the right data, building the test systems, and benchmarking competitors, while all the company's NetWorking strives to develop relationships with key manufacturing customers interested in the project and willing to provide input to the effort. More than 100 customers, excited by the prospects and willing to participate as test sites for the new software, openly share their data with the DR team.

When DR finally releases the new software system, Cybernant, to the marketplace, it revolutionizes the entire robotics industry by providing an uninterrupted nerve link between the customer and the manufacturing floor. Cybernant allows a customer to place an order for a particular item, which instantaneously travels to inventory control where a DR robot fetches or orders all of the parts necessary for building the customers' product, then batches it all in a kit that other robots transport to a location where a human worker assembles the kit. The finished product goes directly to the customer weeks or even months ahead of former schedules.

Because Cybernant moves the customer closer to production, some manufacturing companies eliminate distributors and dealers, going directly to their own customers, increasing their margins, and offering end cusumers lower prices. Other customers gain tremendous increases in the filling of their orders because the new system better links all of the critical activities in the manufacturing process and cuts manufacturing cycle times. As a result, an entirely new approach to manufacturing, with redesigned plant layouts and PCs for every worker, emerges among many of DR's customers.

After two years, Digital Robotics changes its name to Cybernant, which signifies its new expertise in manufacturing information systems. The company now looks more like a software developer than a manufacturer. Although the company still produces robotics systems, that work represents only a small part of the overall company. James Fairmont congratulates you on sticking with your vision to reinvent the company. "It's not only different than I ever imagined," he observes, "it's better." One major customer agrees, "Cybernant will eventually put dealers and wholesalers out of business."

The makeup of the company changes drastically as the predominant skills become software engineering, programming, and information management. The entire culture shifts from PowerWorking engineers and manufacturing mechanics to ValueWorking software developers and manufacturing visionaries.

The new culture is agile, flexible, inventive, and distinctly up-beat. Cybernant leads the explosive growth of the new manufacturing information systems market, and company revenues double in two years. There are projections of even greater growth in the future.

James Fairmont eventually retires and passes the chairmanship on to you. Seven years after taking over as CEO of Digital Robotics, you find yourself leading one of the world's largest information and software systems conglomerates. For Cybernant, the information superhighway has become an intergalactic pathway to the future.

METAWORKING PRINCIPLES FOR ORGANIZATIONS

The three outcomes of this story show that the principles of organizational MetaWorking differ somewhat from those that apply to an individual or team. As you consider these principles, you will see why the various options for Digital Robotics turned out the way they did.

PRINCIPLE 1

Organizational MetaWork emphasizes the right dimension of work at the right time based on developments in the marketplace. Although MetaOrganizations perform work in all three dimensions, they often make one the driving force for a specific situation. Shifting emphasis to another driving dimension at the right time can make all the difference between success and failure.

The Digital Robotics case reveals the importance of emphasizing the right dimension of work at the right time. Option A, with its continuing stress on PowerWork, can lead to marginal success, but shifting to NetWork or ValueWork, because of the changing circumstances in the marketplace, makes more sense.

PRINCIPLE 2

Each dimension of MetaWork can produce positive, yet dramatically different, benefits for an organization.

In the Digital Robotics story, each dimension of MetaWork produced positive results for the company. However, the degree of both immediate and long-term benefits differed greatly as each option unfolded. The PowerWorking emphasis of Option A produced the most immediate benefits for the company, but not as much long-term potential. The NetWorking aim of Option B offered the most benefit in the intermediate term, whereas the ValueWorking thrust of Option C afforded the strongest long-term positioning for the company in the marketplace. Organizational leaders must contemplate the full range of benefits that each dimension will likely produce, and they must match PowerWorking, NetWorking, and ValueWorking to the task at hand, ever ready to shift emphasis when the task at hand changes. As a rule of thumb, PowerWorking gets the best immediate results, NetWorking the best intermediate results, and ValueWorking the best long-term results.

PRINCIPLE 3

Each dimension of MetaWork, when emphasized as the driving force, will take an organization in an entirely different strategic direction, and will result in markedly different organizational and competitive positions. Shifts in work dimensions can drive the most successful strategic and cultural changes.

Each of the options in the Digital Robotics story resulted in different strategies and cultures for the company, and each created its own unique future. Business leaders can accelerate and streamline strategic and cultural change by relying on a work dimension to drive change. Such an approach to organizational change can draw people and processes at all levels into a common understanding and purpose better than any other method of mobilization.

METAWORKING STRATEGIES FOR LEADERS

Organizational MetaWorking begins with an understanding of the company's current work dimension emphasis. To assess your organization's current emphasis and the possible outcomes of stressing different work dimensions in the future, you can use the following questions to begin assessing your organization's circumstances:

- Which, if any, people or functions in the organization currently perform MetaWork?

- Where in the organization does PowerWorking, Net-Working, and ValueWorking currently take place?

- What work dimension dominates organizational decision making and operational focus?

- How will future market characteristics and conditions propel different work dimension emphases?

With answers to these or similar questions in hand, leaders can develop appropriate strategies for increasing MetaWorking, reinforcing or shifting the work dimension emphasis, and shifting the mix and emphasis for the future.

MetaWorking can also help you interpret the fundamental elements that should be weighed when anyone is making strategic decisions. Strategy usually emerges from a consideration of industry characteristics, the nature of the competition, the company's position in the market, and the changing needs of customers. To assist you in making MetaStrategic decisions, use Table 8.1, which illustrates MetaWork responses to a variety of strategic conditions:

Table 8.1. MetaWork responses to different strategic conditions

Factors	Conditions and Responses			
	PowerWork	**NetWork**	**ValueWork**	**MetaWork**
Industry life cycle characteristics	*Declining:* Emphasize efficiency and lower costs.	*Growing:* Form alliances with new partners to continue expanding capabilities.	*Start-up:* Establish a solid position by providing unique value.	*Mature:* Work in all dimensions.
Nature and makeup of competition	*Cut-throat commodity-based:* Become the low cost provider.	*Highly fragmented and localized:* Form alliances and partnerships to dominate regional markets.	*Unstable and confused:* Discover new ways to establish market leadership.	*Stable and entrenched:* Keep the same emphasis in all three dimensions and work to improve each.

Company position and market share	**Eroding:** Recapture position in the short term by redesigning work flow and cutting costs.	**Building:** Form strategic alliances to strengthen position.	**Niche:** Continue to discover value to create opportunities not addressed by competitors.	**Dominant:** Maintain dominant position by working in all dimensions.
Customer trends	**Static and unchanging:** Focus on increasing effectiveness and efficiency of operations.	**Major changes with unclear direction:** Establish a broad base of partnerships and alliances.	**Major changes with clear direction:** Target new value creation opportunities based on changes.	**Constant change:** Excel in all work dimensions.

This MetaStrategy framework provides a powerful tool for thinking and acting according to principle rather than procedure, for focusing on basics rather than fads, and for achieving progress rather than mere activity. Its blueprint for achievement redefines the employer–employee relationship by focusing on work dimensions rather than on jobs, tasks, reporting relationships, compensation, or performance specifications.

For example, the CD-ROM industry looks and feels like it's in the start-up phase of the industry life cycle because everything is still being defined and established. ValueWorking in this industry will pay the biggest dividends in the long term. The software industry appears to be in the growth phase with spectacular successes such as Microsoft, Novell, Lotus, and Broderbund vying aggressively for market dominance, while gobbling up smaller competitors through acquisitions and mergers. In such an industry environment, NetWorking separates the permanent players from the temporary ones because only the companies that can quickly build competence and capability internally and through external acquisition will meet the demands of a growing market. The computer hardware industry, placed by most observers in the mature phase, is full of competitors attempting to maintain a lively balance across a broad spectrum of key variables to remain successful. If they don't, they suffer reversals that mirror IBM's recent woes. Once a company in any industry decides on a work dimension emphasis, it becomes easier for the company to develop management processes, hire employees, and move forward because there are clear answers to the what, how, and why of its efforts.

Only MetaWorking can give a company the band width and focus depth necessary to consistently succeed in a mature industry. In contrast, the typewriter industry represents a declining industry in which companies fight for every possible cost savings and tiny competitive advantage. PowerWorking drives every company in this sort of industry toward greater and greater efficiency and cost effectiveness. Although a high-tech company could conceivably produce products in each of the aforementioned industries, or shift from one to another, it will always benefit from acknowledging the dimension of work that best suits each industry type.

Whether addressing issues of strategic positioning, organizational renewal, or industry life cycles, the executives, managers, and employees in any size or type of organization can apply the principles of MetaWorking to conquer the major challenges of the future: value creation, capability enhancement, motivation, hiring practices, job selection, position description, work design, team effectiveness, training, skill development, evaluation, promotion, reward systems, employee satisfaction, human fulfillment, and talent deployment. Achievements in all of these areas will maximize values for the customer in the new global economy where decentralization, self-directed teams, international markets, technology, and rapid change place ever-increasing pressures on productivity.

As downsizing, delayering, and reengineering programs drive more and more people to launch their own new enterprises where productivity literally determines the life or death of a business, the MetaWork System can help this new wave of value creators to grow and build tomorrow's "best in world" companies. With the principles of MetaWork, entrepreneurs can better address the challenges of capital acquisition, business applications, strategic alliances, resource utilization, talent development, competitive advantage, customer value, and wealth creation by focusing on work dimension management and leadership.

After the Transformation

"Work is much more fun than fun."

Noel Coward

FROM WORKSCAPE TO DREAMSCAPE

Cameron Boyle, founder of Worldpieces, an importer of African art and crafts in New York City, doesn't know the meaning of the word "work." She spends more time traveling to Africa, South America, Asia, and Europe than she does living in Manhattan. "When I graduated from Stanford with a degree in Italian," she recalls, "not many job descriptions fit my resume."

She wanted to go into business and took the advice from Michael Silva, a Salt Lake City-based management consultant, who advised her to study foreign languages and communications rather than conventional business disciplines. As Michael put it, "Young people today are entering a job market where people skills will empower them more than knowledge of finance or marketing."

After graduation, Cameron spent more than a year living in Italy, where she made many friends while attending the Stanford program in Florence. "I fell in love with other cultures," she says, "and you can't get to know people in other countries without knowing their language." Before long, she met a Senegalese businessman, began learning his native language, Wolof, and discovered her dream. "Fama introduced me to African art," says Cameron, "which is so different from Western art. I thought I could find a market for masks, statues, stools, mats and rare bronze pieces in the United States."

Worldpieces hosts showings of contemporary and antique African art in Palm Beach, New York, and Boston, where Americans can buy, at wholesale prices, ethnographic and tribal art imported from several African countries. Cameron runs her business with some principles they don't teach you at the Harvard Business School. As she explains, "I always try to substitute the word 'dream' for the word 'work.' It's so much more fun to say "I'm going to dream today,' or 'I did a lot of dreaming today.' Even when I take on a research assignment at Goldman Sachs to make ends meet, I try not to think of it as work but as adding to my ability to make my own dreams come true."

Like Lyle Anderson, whom we met earlier, Cameron has learned to think and act in a way that enhances her performance every day, by using the three-dimensional model—doing, developing and discovering—but she applies it through what she calls the three Fs. "My upbringing taught me to concentrate on what's really important in life. For me, that's Family, Faith, and the Future. By family I mean all the important people in my life—my parents, my brother, my husband, my husband's family, my friends, and my business associates. Without their support and help, I can accomplish nothing. Faith means both my faith in myself and my faith in God. And everything I do creates my future."

Cameron Boyle has chosen the path of the MetaWorker. Like Stephen Snell, whom we met in the Prologue, a great deal of her life involves work (or, as she would put it, "dreaming"), and she has embarked on a personal program to realize her dreams. It can also happen for you.

Whether you dream of creating greater financial success, obtaining deeper spiritual well-being, designing the proverbial better mousetrap, curing a deadly disease, or simply achieving a richer life with more liberty and greater happiness, it all begins and ends with you. No one else can make your dreams come true.

Once you seize control of your own destiny, no one can get in your way. As William Worrime observes in this poem from his little book, *101 Corporate Haiku:*

> Thorns block my pathway
> to the sunlight—the thousand
> little managers.

Nicely put, but heaping the blame for unacceptably low productivity on the failings of management skirts the real issue: Only individuals wield the power to enhance productivity. To begin your own unique journey toward fulfilling your dreams, look not to others, be they managers, co-workers, family members, mentors, or teachers. Look in the mirror and ask yourself one question: "Have I fallen into the trap of believing that I am entitled to success, well-being, and a fulfillment of my dreams just because I showed up on this planet?" Such an assumption will send anyone down the primrose path to failure.

With the MetaWork System, we have proposed a concrete program that all can use to transform themselves, their teams, and their organizations toward unprecedented achievement. Mastering it may not result in a utopia, but it can, we believe, push each and every one of us into the fourth dimension, where MetaWorkers from all walks of life deliver the results, competence, and breakthroughs that the future demands.

SUPERACHIEVEMENT FOR ALL

Many, if not most, of the world's great family fortunes, business empires, governmental achievements, technological advancements, philosophical triumphs, and artistic contributions trace their origins to periods of revolutionary change. Likewise, the WorkScape revolution promises great rewards to those who adapt wisely and well to the new world of work.

Novelist and commentator, H.G. Wells, often said that modern men and women are engaged in a race between education and catastrophe. We doubt if he could have imagined how difficult that race would become at the end of the twentieth century. More than any earlier era in human history, our times call for a clearer understanding of the principles of individual, group, and organizational performance, not simply for the sake of monetary gain, security, or personal advantage, but for the well-being of society itself.

Through our combined collection of more than 75 years of consulting engagements, management interviews, strategy sessions, off-site retreats, corporate culture assessments, conference workshops, business writing, and book publishing, we have worked in thousands of intensely focused, time-condensed situations in which people have grappled with the most fundamental questions of their organizational and personal lives. The same questions invariably arise: "What goal justifies all of our strivings to improve our productivity?" "Does our performance really matter in the end?" "Are we accomplishing anything of lasting worth?" Although the answers never come easily, the struggle to answer such questions has always confirmed our belief that work does matter, and that it can make a difference in peoples' lives, teams, and organizations. In our hearts, we believe that working in the fourth dimension can make all the difference in the world.

Index

For More Information

If you would like more information about how to move yourself, your team, or your organization into the Fourth Dimension and the next level of achievement, please contact

MetaWork Systems, Inc.
50 South Main #25, Suite 18
Salt Lake City, Utah 84144
801-355-META (6382)

MetaWork Systems, Inc. currently offers a one day seminar designed to help people implement the principles, processes, and practices of the MetaWork System in all aspects of their personal and professional work. Specific information about the MetaWork Journal, self-paced learning programs, and electronic/multi-media versions of the MetaWork System is available upon request.

About the Authors

Craig Hickman is the best-selling author of *The Productivity Game, The Organization Game, The Strategy Game, The Oz Principle, Mind of a Manager, Soul of a Leader, Creating Excellence, The Future 500,* and other influential books and articles. After graduating with honors from the Harvard Business School, he worked as a strategic planner for the Fortune 500 company Dart Industries and later became a director of strategic management consulting at Arthur Young & Company, now Ernst & Young, where the four co-authors of *The Fourth Dimension* first worked together. As an independent management consultant, he currently conducts workshops for businesses and management groups worldwide; serves as a member of the board of directors of APS Holding, one of the largest automotive parts distributors in the United States; and is Editor-in-Chief of *Utah Business* magazine.

Craig Bott is Chairman and CEO of MetaWork Systems, a training and consulting firm devoted to implementing the concepts described in *The Fourth Dimension* as a means of helping people and organizations achieve greater results, competence, and breakthroughs in their work. He is a former Vice President of Corporate Productivity Services at Franklin Quest, the $200 million developer and marketer of the Franklin Day Planner, a time and productivity management tool. Prior to that he was a principal with Arthur Young & Company, now Ernst & Young, where he directed projects in the areas of strategic management, competitive benchmarking, competitive analysis, continuous improvement, and organizational development. He received his master's degree in management from Brigham Young University.

Marlon Berrett is an independent businessman and consultant involved in several high-growth business enterprises, including

Assist International, a fast-growing financial software development company, where he is formulating growth plans for domestic and European markets. After completing his MBA at Indiana University, he joined Arthur Young & Company, now Ernst & Young, where he eventually opened their Salt Lake City office and became Managing Partner of the firm's management consulting practice in the Intermountain West. He has consulted with numerous businesses, government organizations, law firms, and not-for-profit organizations in a variety of industries, serving as partner-in-charge of hundreds of engagements during his 21 years with Arthur Young & Company. He has won praise throughout the United States for his professional leadership on sensitive public issues and management studies of health care, utilities, and public organizations.

Brad Angus is the President of Northfield John Deere, a group of John Deere dealerships in the western United States. After serving as a navigator in the United States Air Force for six years and receiving his MBA from New Hampshire College, Brad joined Little & Company, an *INC.* 500 firm with revenues of $5 million, as Vice President of Operations. He later moved to Arthur Young & Company, now Ernst & Young, as a management consultant, where he became manager of strategic management consulting services. Prior to his current position, he was President of ATK motorcycles, the leading U.S. manufacturer of off-road sporting bikes, where he redesigned the company's manufacturing system and supplier network.